MW00713067

Poison Mash

by Myra Fairchild

For Millie Fairchild Adcot

Designed by Michael R. Eddy

Printed in the United States of America

Library of Congress Control Number: 2006933578

ISBN   0-9789453-0-1
          978-0-9789453-0-5

I dedicate this book to my husband Bob Fairchild for his unwavering support, faith, and unconditional love.

I also include my Father who is now at rest but who always told me I was a writer and who offered tidbits of wisdom which have never been rivaled.

I offer my best wishes to my beautiful, gifted daughter Tara Himler who encourages me in all my endeavors and to my adorable grandsons Alexander and Riley who are always uplifting as all I need to do is look at their photo to get happy, joyous feelings of grit and ridiculously positive thoughts of freedom and hope for the future.

I extend my special thanks to my best friend from childhood, Roselynn Motsch, who is always happy and supportive.

Special thanks to Mike Raymond Eddy who suggested the title be "Poison Mash" and who designed the cover of the book.

The photo of me was taken by Ken Ross himself in the 1980's and prior to his death.

ABOUT THE AUTHOR

Myra Fairchild began writing at an early age and has written poetry all her life. She has attended school all her life and been involved in all manner of making art from cooking to painting, designing ways to use or recycle old clothing, and found objects.

Having grown up in the country on a farm, she understands the importance of using everything in its entirety and believes in eating home-grown food, growing free-range chickens, and farming. To quote her parents, "It is so important for us to be good stewards of the environment. We should never be guilty of wasting the wonderful water afforded us, polluting the soil, nor abusing the air." The air, land, and water work in tandem and the earth is a living organism and must be treated with respect in order that it continue to live.

Myra was active in Summer Theatre and attended Yarmouth Summer Theatres as a youngster. She was a participant in several community theatres as an actress.

Myra studied painting from Charles Bell who painted portraiture of Hollywood actors such as Paul Roberson and he designed the first fiberglass boats for Shell Oil.

In 2004, Myra, with her husband Bob, took his father's cheese knife to market and now sells it through their company, Fairchild Tech Associates, LLC.

Myra spent a great deal of time traveling when the world was still glorious and open and full of lively human beings . . . She wonders often what has gone so wrong and if the present population is asleep.

Poison Mash

Poetry & Musings

there was this kid in drama class   whose ear lobes hung down

so far,   alas

he'd tuck them into his ear canals

        and clasping his chin he'd pop them out.

brides don't have insides they're too perfect

        always aglow with saccharine

    their distinction   their demise

    corpses don't have insides   they're too gone

  like brides   their insides have nested

    while their machinery rested

Vienna sausages or walking blobs . . . what French

sounds like in Mississippi

I taught you how not to be guilty
                    and bore your labor with the pain.
          I saw your child at the mouth of birth
                         and held your back when it hurt
Something happened . . .
                    you changed and went into the pit.
   you met me with a cold blue stare
                    and kept your affection for shabby things.
when time has seen you humble
                         that choice belongs to everyone,
          I wonder what you'll remember
                         when the world is down to one.

the tv was on and the interview was going about the prince and he
was surrounded by arabs in formal attire . . . you know dish rags
and robes.

          one of them picked a big booger and promptly
plopped it into his mouth.

have you seen what living does

        the old man used to laugh, dance over logs

                      in his

need to find happy things . . . ate with a knife even peas

            and fried everything in olive oil.

he lived that way   not gentle.

              death came, the reaper

                and the

shroud.

        black fell across his old gray face. smothering he did

in the darkness but

I know the swift soul that slit the grave like a polished

Steel knife

      and I heard his song split upward through the night.

the garage door, my kitchen floor and polished doesn't wait.

           I like it most waxed

childhood ghost, I think I'll take a skate.

the ptomaine smile returns   the need for death, resigning. . .
standing in   rows, headstones posed, sale made, signing.
A birth certificate, an opening, one bed free with a window, then
hands gone empty,
running, fingers screaming, working, madness knotting
backward jerking,
           Oh, not for you, embracing,   my need still crawls racing
and the inability to live.

today I am crisp   someone will bite me and I will crack
brittle   all over   then they'll sweep up the
triangle pieces into a small
scoop   to be turned into a brown bag
which will find it's way into a big truck   full of
everyone else's debris   me

when I return I will be different   change does not happen
with caution   I must commit this sin and with passion
          sanity only permits reality … her high blown arrogance
I ate a purple hyacinth and died

We planted ten rain tree SEEDS

tonight.................the hummingbird sat on the outdated tv antenna
and bob watered

his tomatoes

Sunday last was father's day

I don't know what was ailing me and then
I remembered Daddy passed just last October
and so I had to remember why I run around all the time with a
toothpick stuck

in my pocket ....my t-shirt pocket mostly

and why I am bossy and walk like

I've got the world by the tail.
I had to remember that my definitive nature is a genetic charm

and my fiery temper which servers to annoy
everyone came upon me long before I exited my mother's womb
and so I thought of my
mercurial disposition   ambition   my file of interests
and my nearly
perfect nose

it was pollard where mother and raeburn made candy

..........world war two divinity...carmels ...sweet stickies

.........rolled in nuts............stardust and always............the

promise that their men would come home.....................maybe

is a bowl wearing a blanket considered a covered dish?

KEOSTLER!!!! what the hell is order?

Imperfection, striving, invention, evolution,

consequence,   or as Einstein said nothing changes

until something moves.

For I am a pilgrim, my highway is star paved and many galaxies I have known.

my babies live in California where the cracks are.............my heart
is   in a   hope basket?

I said I wanted more. You listened. You said you were grateful for what you had. I listened. Because you listened and said what you said and because I listened and

heard   I have more.

the price of excellence is great. . . the tax evolved appreciates. Those who have it

pay in stall ments.................statements in freakdom.

my skin is thin, that's why I've been afraid to cry or laugh or die

here we are on highway 10   again   headed for buckeye.....bored
     stupid............
          Brown grass   tired ass   green signs
          dead minds

I saw you coming back to me in my white dress, night hair.
I ran to you in abandon, leaving everything in quiet............
                  vast............a pilgrim in all.

who is the person I'm with, she's hollow.
                I feel like cutting her open
to see if she has an aorta or a lattisimus dorsi.
        maybe she is ill and needs surgery. She
has no heart and her   stomach is full of pebbles.

peter, peter, I can't fly, I have diamonds in my eye.

   Leaden head,   neutered ear,   darning hearts is my career.

Leave your burden,   Peter, fly.

                   Know what songs the swallows cry.

Out of 100%, the article said, 65 to 71% were old. 39% were
Hispanic, 34% were white, 50% were Hispanic Children, 12.7%
were Asian, 28% were black, with 12% over
65 by 2020. What does it all mean?

it's mellow here, queer, how a tree is a play these days,

                             or anticipating

another shadow cast and asleep on a rock that is entertainment
enough.

Don't bring your petty one ups man shit here. It hurts my eyes.

Mother's day 1993 I spent with a dust mask, 14 brooms,

     and two men, one of whom repeated every word I said.
"Oh," I said, "this is really nasty." "OH," he said, "this is really
nasty."
Nothing like edification.

When last I caressed Riley, he just said, "that's my magic ear". my
heart curved, my soul beat. What a child, what a child.

E.D. and S.T., R.F. and Edgar Guest. R.B. and E.C.C., M.M. and
Tennyson. W.J.B and T.S.E Gee

the animal circus has come to town dressed in tents of pink and
brown.

I went to UGU, the underground university and everyone got a
degree even me

he feels as though he's been ambushed by a flowering shrub. What
fun. It's a pun

He propped the door with his knee and balanced the box on top so
I could pass through with my load of mail.
She stopped as I passed through
 and smiled, dropping her lids at him. "Oh, you're holding the
door for me".   boney assed bitch.

I am ice and move in drips
upon the floor of earth my lips   press bruise on bruise
in fossil pain,   around a globe my sweat doth rain. The
sticky earth behind me dries,   the septic life before me dies, I
am blue or ptomaine green,   the light doth make me
everything.
    In sun, I spill a yellow bowl, at dusk my edge is filmed in gold.
my glazes spill from tented nights
                        and turn my wanton nature white, In fire,
I'm Alpha, Eden's twin,   then come Omega
                Omega, when?

This is for weeds or seeds (drawing). These are also legs or warts or holes.

This price is so great, all this hurt and this hate, I am tearing and wringing about.

This confusion deletes me, it kills and defeats me, it strangles me,

too, with such doubt.. I suffer alone,

I've no love and no home, I'm an invalid tied to my head.

Just give me some rest,

let me off from your test

free me now from your strangling grasp.

Time is a presumption conjured up by mundane ordinances

Didn't know about scrimshaw til I saw that raccoon.
      All those beautiful lines mined from cool ivory.
How could anything so elegant   properly embrace a raccoon.
          The moon hung like an ivory ball
the first night I spied those criminal eyes and peered into that
            world of unduplicated orneriness

all those ups and downs were an instead route to the same
destination.
      Everyone is here, just like Disneyland. I'm disappointed.
All that comradery was a something else
      and companero is just a fancy name. Having rested, I'm
ready to leave
with the enlightenment that I'll never choose this route again.
      The reward isn't worth the effort. It's more subtle
than that. I could have
      had an overview instead of dying on the color

given the world is, I have not seen enough of sky wedges or birds
and trees roosted against a painted drop.   played out
passion sky, summer dusk,

                              you grip a bloody epitaph
strung like floral fashion or a golden hope, thrumming a lover's
little death, a dreamer's
last goodbye............................ I ....have not seen
enough of
wonders rocking in the moon hours, draped in star fabric. . .

        age drips in iambic importance while dreams soak out white
in the deep long night.

                But in the rush home there is a fever now seeping
salt and hurt through this debris. Me.

                              and morning comes and on and one,
                                        I go to the sun.

Predawn on an Amtrak train.

            Yelling at the coffee stand, shit on the toilet seat.

                                    finally, silence.

            then back up, go forward, back up, go forward.

Leaving New Orleans

Fat people, mash potato ass, cost of fuel, air travel, religious right.
What a fright.

It's really hard to live with so much loneliness. I understand how it
must be for old folks, forgotten, shriveled, left to a pet or tv meal for
one

Have you ever visited the in-between where the grass is BLUE and
the sky is GREEN.
where the trees all grow up a side ways knoll and you fall through
the ground instead of a hole.
I visited a place that was half-way out of the in between place on
the in between route
and the moon bent and kissed me when my visit was done and the
clouds poured honey from a bowl of sun.

Colonel Blimp, an elderly, pompous, short-sighted reactionary
lived with Colly wobbles or pains in the stomach

I have a talent for finding beautiful, magical, elusive wonders but I
don't want to own, keep on hold; I don't have a need to pervert
with ownership. Experience and freedom are the genesis of what is
worthwhile. The drive to own anything has never rendered me but
tears. Why would I want to halt the stars from dancing.
Thoughts about Susan

And he lived amidst prosaic utterances,
                         shadows pasted against a backdrop of
mechanical habits, a seraglio of stilted possibility,   but they
did not seduce him
nor was he caught going Friday nights to the juice factory
and looking to the Wednesday participation at the meat market,
his frayed prayer floated, bleated occasionally, and sang about
injustice.
              No one listened and God laid out another male child this
other palm Sunday.

Below the raft the water ripples

                    creating a small but busy stir.

above the raft   the wind whispers

         talking a weird but pleasant whirr.

the raft drifts onward   complacently   all alone in the
midst of the sea. then

      suddenly from atop the sky comes a violent wind with a

                vicious cry.   the water below
begins to rage, in the life

          of the raft, fate turns a page.
racking and crashing, plunging and ripping, the little raft, turning
and dipping,

      faster and faster it tumbles and tosses knowingly
nodding for each of its losses.

From out of the depth comes a quiet breeze, crying, crying,

          "please no please.

          I could never have conquered this sea
for it sucked this life fast out of me.   And so it be my epitaph,

     'there is not much glory for being a raft'"

Compressed and compounded, I'm full and I'm rounded, I've been
eating donut holes.

What color is hurt?

What is its texture? Is it black and lumpy or white and sun yellow?   Neither afford staring into, the pain is too great. . .

lost in the black or rendered sightless from the rays.

Does its mileage gather from scaling mounds or become endless in its monotony.

It just hurts and deep steeps like black or drops white in sun yellow hot

The same road again, the same hour, mind peeled, discipline, work, goals, frustration.   Stay here now, now stay here.   The leaves shift, sift, gold in the sun, waiting, choke, spew, toss against blue, the same hour again, the same season, earth peeled,

nature, cruel, the wheel

Bully, bully, Mr. Unruly, Teddy Bear Roo Velt. Patience

The tree bleeds green in my front yard and rose of Sharon
angles hard against the glass behind my head.

Mahler travels through the house and flings his sound
across the road where Mothers in pale pinafores munch peanut
butter pie
and I alone buzz and groan a symphony into the phone.

tumbling about me crashing and breaking that's how I die.

like a caving mountain, thunder ripping the sky.
every tumble bruises, each crack heaves a scream, belching forth at
random,

how I make the scene.

leave my freedom caring, judge my being not,

we're in the womb of heaven, evolving is our lot

the God in you, the God in me, the God in us, is the God I see.

Lines on a globe, precision. decision.   lines turn circles
somehow,   don't they?

you creep along, you slimy worm, you have no brain, you cannot learn, you feel no pain, you are no worse, you thrive on dirt, you drill the soil,

you have no grief, nor any toil. Your life is endless, this is your fate,   your ignorance eternal,

you regenerate

I am a flower, still, I am Sabra,

though my perfume is fading, my neck droops a little and my stem grows weak. Still..............I am a flower,

alone

in my autumn   garden.

There are no other blooms to mute my glorious color, no barbed rose to malign my dignity, nor sweet violet left to remind me of spring.

No passer by will harm me. I am only one, alone in my own profusion.

The lights are all out for his erection, he's getting it on with my sextion; meanwhile, he thinks I'm some buttered broad with under arm green beans.   Life is so pristine

Spook juice roils and rivulets through me like water in a kettle
bound for boiling over and I am all set to walk and wonder, woof
and tweeter, at the morning hour, alone in my life of leftovers and
half eaten orcs on their way to extinction. my little dog laughs ugly
        sometimes he looks at me with his
         mouth arc scissored into a nasty smile,
his smile looks like it was set with pinking sheared teeth.
he growls and dances a little gigue when he sees the fire hydrant
thinking piss on the corner of the golf course, the jolly green place
where guys fart and gesture.
Sad but true, what to do,
      as the world fills up with grotesque, grinning politics
polyester, pus mongers hoarding bank accounts and the NYSE
future wins at the expense
of some poor idiot who thought he'd retire with nothing
    to do but drink spook juice
        and fart on the fire hydrant.

And so I walk the black forest, me and my nemesis.
i hear sounds others are not privy to and hurts swell in my woman
gut.
     I have learned to be tough and silent in my turn to destiny.
i do not yawl at the grim reaper or the devil's horn
nor is angst let forth when I see fences
       where the gate is gone

Riley and I were out playing baseball with a plastic bat and ball.

I was pitching and he was poised with his bat in the air

and I said, "keep your eye on the ball, Riley"

                and he made a circle with his thumb

        and forefinger   like that

and put it over his eye and looked through at me not saying a word.

        I sat down on the concrete play area and wept.

I am a white American, opaque,

        I have no charge accounts like those of the jews,

    the blacks, red and yellow, I pay up in neat installments.

not granted an hour of self-pity, my Mother lives and amid gardens

of spring flowers.

        she loves her bonsai tree. It has gone on for years

that way. Nor have I cried for my country. not those tears, I am an

American, white, opaque. how should I care about a country.

        there are no countries, just people assigning

importance to sounds and documents, departmentalizing,

intellectualizing, defining,

        specializing.

the ability to think has never been important so why be busy here.

I don't know, I'll never know, I am an American, white. 1997

When we move, it's always so fast, no time to think or reflect on
anything.

just poking paper around treasures thrust quickly into
cartons.   All the high moments lost in white tissue paper,
christmas, births, deaths, weddings, new friends, new jobs, more
residences, dust left

over the window ledge, a special knob found
in an antique emporium or

the pepper tree we watched grow from a sapling
now tall and holding its own. I am holding on, looking back at all
the houses I've left, little apartments, dwellings like smells telling a
once loved friend or a ghost visiting me to say, "It is necessary
to redo a moment or two . . . something lost during the parade". I
leave the trees and strong bulbs grown tougher by division and
replanting,   yes, leaving an old hole for a new home in the soil,
a poor plant to root somewhere else . . . torn and moved to a new
residence

One orange will suffice, that is nice

I don't need a crate, only to eye it,
smell it, pretend to squeeze it,   I'll pay as much for
that good orange, then take it home and eat it.

Aside from the fact that she was a beautiful girl with eyes the size of small tea saucers and that she was physically gifted with her queen size udders, she was just my very best friend and I'd welcome her wonderful smell in the heat standing there in the sun with judges eyeing us. She would get tired and lay her head on my shoulder and later on she broke my heart, her baby drying up inside her swollen belly and the vet was there and they wouldn't let me go to her and I know how she wanted me with her as she lay dying without me holding her head. It would have been ok for her blood to cover me or stain my clothes. Wendy's blood was all over me when she gave birth to Brea Ann and she was only human, not at all like my dear cow whom I adored. I had no idea how I would hurt these many years later remembering the smell of the old barn and the fear in my heart as they kept me from her and she died at the farm, the farm I love. When I love, it is like the heavens open up and smother the world in blossoms and a little smell of earth, just a tiny thing as big as baby doll's giant lashed brown eyes, big with love and pleading,

"help me, please"

nothing is open when you get up early, not even your eyes, but as Thomas   used to say. . . the birds are out walking

in the streets at 4:00am.

The world growls and howls at its prey as she brings a bloody heart
to her teeth, the pain is gone soon but   I
wonder why I Had to see it and could do nothing to save the head
full of promise. I've watched them as

      they trip, waste away in desperation, or gather in the field at
the turnstile, turning, going, never coming back from the impotent
fields. their lives rotten in a field of hope and manure. . . then. . .

        in a week,

          occasional wild flowers bloom and open and the
world smiles

        the night is black and deep. I can't sleep.

         my eyes like search lights blinking,
I keep thinking.

    The sun winks at my head and now I want to go to bed.

we went to lunch wanting to know one another
over cheese, eggs, pasteurized conversation

feeling our way through grease and details.

you talked about your brother's homosexuality, death

we'd just experienced a friend's successful suicide . . .
"pass the jelly. Do I offend you with my cigarette, more coffee".
I wonder what my insides would be like washed and soaked.
would black grime bubble up

belching through soap bubbles. Sump, fill me up.
we forgot we were remembering and I saw your blue eyes register
data . . .

another reporter you said blow by blow description. I'm
dead, telling you my secrets.   The toast is gone, hash
brown pressboard.

do you like women I asked, something awful about your
Mother. We decided we were born alcoholics, your bro, born gay,
the mark of the cow, needing a drink

from a pool infested with dead insects
and she filled her belly already fetus grown . . . what does a Mother
do, who, has given forth a God's oddling. We finished, said our
goodbyes, another time to meet now that the formalities have been
dealt with we can get on to the

after birth

She was telling me about a friend of hers who had a baby and they named it Blueberry . . . it all seemed so in character for Tara to have a friend who named her baby Blueberry.....................It was after that Tara went off to Australia to be with her waterloo and his grandmother had a best friend there and her name was Mrs. Beanstalk. Tara told me to never mention it, and of course I would not. "Don't mention it, Mom," she said, pursing her lips and making those dimples she had that played all around her perfect mouth. "They recently took Mrs. Beanstalk away."

It was a serious morning and my new son in law was sitting out under the porch roof quietly reading the paper. He said Tara had called Butterfinger and Butterfinger to ask about having some art pieces appraised. It is so hard to be serious sometimes with my daughter and her new "man" who is as pretty as she is.

I see my child beyond the top of the rise to conquer the summit.
                    She stops to check her time piece and
                         bows in the wind. I go with my
cheek angled against
                    the wind and don't care when the moon is
full of mist or blood.
               I have accepted living along the pow wow trail and I
have seen my brothers
          torn to nothing but forever I will love my daughter
through the tribulation

he stood with his thumbs stuck in his back pockets and he blew out
first one side and then the other of the corners of his mouth
               and then he shook that sweet head,
                    looked down, and said,
"I picked em up, I turned em around, I put em down, and there
they are."

Today it is strange and very odd, to think of God. 9-11

we are greeted with the surprise that the sea reclaimed the city

built on a sand bar

while george bush speaks of treating them all like family?

good grief, whose family, his or mine? Not on my watch.

and then he went on to say: This is a very serious,

important job. What a surprise.

This is sweet and sour pork, Jack,

those coffins you refer to which never get wet

the folks in Loozyanna and the deep are getting real wet,

popping up in their watery graves;

goofballsillypomes – I'm sure your coffin is dry,

bone dry and silly with pomes.

I found that piece of quilting Mary Caroline had done.

she is always laughter and happiness,   a person who makes

me feel light

and free. Mary has no care for material things.

Everything Mary

possesses is in her face.

The touch of a lip is soft, scintillating, secrets slipped from the
bee's bountiful bouqueting of buzzing boredom,

          morning's mysterious longing left like a kiss
on the glowing hours   assurance of certain pleasures pout
poised silent sins

           exquisite evenings long making little murders in
the love leveled meadowed mellow hay mow life ago youth touch
of a lip soft suggesting the tide

         movement mounting in fantastic fleeting ecstasy
near the inside folds of her sighing thighs.

they talk about cars, I am permitted to listen. I listen. I learn
about birth, engine powered birth, polyester lined wombs
connected up with extruded polyethylene
and moltened other resins turning it over

         warming it up oil the gears so the shift won't stick.
She clips along at a good pace, held on the road by his expertise.
she needs grease. I listen. They talk about cars.

      I go to my room to apply manufactured lubricants,
         just like polymer poultices, in every orifice.

in July, the firecrackers sing

and lemonade steeps and grows warm,

the air is damp and the nights are hot

and the wizard knows what the owl sees.

in July, the fireflies dance, rains come hard from

plumped gray clouds,

green apples hang on the lush green boughs,

and

children know what the owl sees.

in July, the fairies are born and they romp for the

newness of things,

the wooded glens are full of them all dressed in their gossamer gowns

and they

already know what the owl sees

Oh, in July the best is come, it's a time the hardy enjoy

and the life there prevails and the Gods all hail

cause they know what the owl sees.

25 words or less,   where I want to go, why I want to go

there, what a mess.   We would like to visit and observe the

habitat of the maine timber doodle and   watch it boogie

through the soft, pleasing, wooded light of the winter brush.

For Sabra: by invitation only, you gave me entrance in, I blew

upon your lovely mast and

bowed to kiss your hand..

Although

you go before me into the fearful black, because my

heart adores you, I'll follow with my faith. there are no

thankful passages nor wonders anymore,

I'll wait and pray for

wisdom at this the reaper's door. my life has lost its promise, a

heart for a tedious slave, I see the   crimson garland, wound

loosely round your grave.

Oh, lonely pillowed

pinioned hurt,

I ache to hold your face, to see you laugh and bend in mirth

at this unerring fate.

for those of us who never hurt,

is sanctioned pleasant days, of carefree hours steeped in rest

and visions of a fair tale.   t'is harder, yes, to

climb the hill where rocks are strewn and rubble cast.

to rise above the crest of pain, to really see, at last.

then lo, the child who dreams himself beyond the thorn or perfect

still,

his heart will tear when those before have learned to climb the hill.

Autumn is a time of remembrance,

a time when beauty reigns supreme,

autumn's cloak of red and gold

shelters the warmth of summer's green.

her sun is warm with undue heat, her breath is cool at night,

her trees rise up with spicy scents,

her moon grows large with harvest light.

beneath her periwinkle sky, her beauty grows as time goes by,

her chief ingredient is a part of mellowed sadness from last year's

heart.

the babe lay clad in cotton, a child with elegant feet, his hands like

flowers bearing forth an endless possibility.   the

lady bent and cradled him against her noble breast. He smiled

and slept inside her arms,

a future world at rest.

you were black and blue that day I found you sitting straight up

against a support timber.   you must have been afraid

of what rigor mortis would do to you   to you

and you pointed the gun

away

from that door   through your temple knowing

I would not see how the needle came through the other side

The fabric of your lovely brain spewed

like a Jackson Pollock   dribble down the concrete blocks and my

awareness   where do I put the rage she asked

It comes at odd hours scribbled on paper napkins

and used envelopes   twenty years of mourning glossed

over with polite utterances

how can I tell what might be brewing until I am all

used up,

completely shorn and drained,

naked at my desk

Out of ink

we raked dried grass into piles heaping it

                around newly planted trees, you and me

         with my heart in a rack.

      each time I looked at you pulling your garden wagon,

a part of my soul died. then I thought about meeting you

somewhere distant and dreamy, someplace God said we could go.

I wondered if you'd

 be wearing your khaki garden clothes then I missed your old

          rubber boots, the ones you wore some years back at

5:00am when you milked the cows,

               before you left for a construction job.

It was a while ago before our eyes were sad and our hearts

       were so heavy. . . It was recess for a moment

       and I was a little girl again wishing you were home

     so Mother wouldn't worry and I could go to sleep.

you'd come from work full of bloody stories . . . Big John fell

from the scaffolding or some other comrade had gone swiftly bent

and dead. I remember, too, those times in the haymow,

    the smell of clover dialing upward,

            dragging a bale to a pitcher in the old barn or

              campfires late at night on the summer lawn.

we sang then, do you remember?

You will always be inside my thinking and your courage will

always give me pride and strength.

I came from a King's loins – a man who knew greatness

          and love that championed the gods.

the treasures of Monterey bay: over caverns and washes

      your long forehead stretches, peering down

           where the water is wide;

racking and breaking   a cacophony making, pregnant with food

    from the tide. Tumbling and dipping,

    your long body ripping, spaces where trees have stood,

     changing and mangled, your beauty unchallenged,

      you sing and you roar about life.

    the sun comes crawling with your labor and yawling

         spreading color and light o'er your face;

    and the world does penance as you beckon and grimace

calling out about struggles and might.

         days go on as you whisper and yawn,

and the sun drops hues on your grace, what splendor you give with

your anger and wit

         like a god breathing soul into space.

It's a gift to be in this place by the sea,

          this story of terror and play,

        there is no where, on earth's grand stair

       like the stages of Monterey bay.

how is it you can laugh raising my soul secrets in lilting shrill

surprises,

you stand still and sizzling in my startled

garden posturing polyester at my Johnny pop ups, pussy pleasure

parading your pocket picks

where are your flowers fucking feisty fluted

stamen sticking stoic dumblike plastic poor.

you have them hidden deep in your perfect, protracted person

charading shadow behind your dancing eyes, surprise, surmise your

lies glad in clown feet, wink like twinkles dimpled

wrinkles at the hour of my

demise

Christmas cookies will never taste the same.

It has been a year of horror.

women and men in America have become so fat they

have to buy the bigger,

up-graded airline seats in order to get one big

enough to fit their big asses into. . .

I watch them at restaurants with elbows on the table, face in the

plate. . . It's the big feed.

gobble, gobble, gobble.

Written for Tara, Winter, 1973

She is Diddle, I am Broom, In our glee, we leave our room

We ride a teddy to softer places, through dancing eyes and pansie faces,

She is my darling, I her slave, in a chocolate boat, we rock a bye wave,

For her delight I dream a whale with a cookie body and a peppermint tale,

Then on we go in our candy sea, Diddle and Broom, the two are we

We land in a place of billy goats, we dine on milk and musical oats

The oats in a form of cherry treats are good for nothing but lovely to eat,

After a nap we meet a goat, with a golden head and a star on his throat

He asks Diddle from whence she came, and really but really if it wasn't a game

Please, he inquires, if we'll whistle a tune, he will transport us back to our room,

We do as he asks and quicker than light, he is transformed into a beautiful knight.

So diddle and Broom now live in a place, full of beauty and love and grace

But their favorite trick makes a magical goat

He's a golden Billy with a star on his throat.

Deya of Mallorca, 1967

      trees, pregnant with lemon, the gnarled legs of the olive,

that way, twisted.

                 sea and sky, blue cup of horizon, goat

bells, nostalgia, bother bruce with flute, pan, this song of Deya

Adam's Sentence: the sunshine smells are worms warming to
shrunken seeds on the cement, rain sated surface

and roses pedaling their pink
soiled presence into boiling essence of docks full of fetid fumes
billowing off trash baskets of fish garments glowing in the
rotting dancing day.
growing globs of glorious algae thrum, thrum, thrum alive
with silver simmer as they stench their way
through the stagnant blush punctuated with clabbered bread bits
belching at the edge of the wasted pacific presence
in the dying passion of the drunken moorings drum, drum,
drumming away.
a man moves his hungry hands across his fisherman flattened
breasts and views the early vista of stone sentences stenciled onto
cemetery structures high above the humous gladdened gardens
where ravens squawk and defecate. Somewhere in the ether, Adam
stands
sentenced to centuries of sunshine smells
and maddening beatitudes albeit creation.

the sound of ticking. some have mute faces. desperate, killing time.
killing. They also die trying to count,   figure it out,
hasten, fast, desperate, killing time, killing
and time simply is without counting

She is drowning in cynicism

           and life strikes the moment while even

in the darkness she exudes beauty, substance, light dances

across her personhood and passers by are armed with that

vision,

even the street signs bend in the wind

          and for one moment there she is free of negativity

and the world is not diminished.

I had to go out today

       and clean the snails from the concrete entrance here, at the

apartment from hell.   A book could not tell what this is all about.

I could not break the little shells away   and I could not

sweep them from my broom. what was I supposed to do, kill

them?

Then the old lady next door called over and wanted me to clean her

       patio and light bulb. what an idea, I was in no mood

for her, what was I supposed to do, kill her?

I died today.

  I always die on sunny afternoons when everyone is so angry,

       even the snails won't give up their grip.

what am I supposed to do, kill them?

Out here the ocean dances,   waves at me in my muddy dress,

peace, I turn turn a human churn   bored and intelligent.

    I get another chance, glance, remember a few days have gone

        since you let me peek at your fresh, new life,

           teeming with exciting things.

For a moment it was I young again, never mind what followed,

going home to see my father wave at me in my muddy dress. I'm

broke, he said, my

          mother's doleful eyes bled, my soul curved, a

concave well, I had to leave, too

     early in my borrowed car, running to catch a plane

back near into what I call heaven. I sat at the bar with my coke

wondering how bitters might taste before I swelled and swallowed.

    2 minutes to flight.

    I grabbed my heart, planted on a bar stool elevator,

my body went along in my muddy dress with my mother's prayers

         and a boarding pass stuck sideways

      in a convoluted ice cream box

it's been a most awful time.

I bend my head, bow my knee, and
pull about my ears in an ongoing vehemence not
understanding what the

real bete noir truly is . . . just life.
I suppose aside from the family malady, impetuous diatribes, and
uncomely situations,

I've just learned that my dear Sabra has Alzheimer's.
she is only 52 and is rapidly progressively more confused, can't
even
count money. My heart has evaporated and I think I have entered
some   second dimension.

People sit around, eat and yak, yak, yak. We all go buy things
and posture.

Meanwhile, amid all this idiocy is reality.

Is this stupid behavior a defense, a front, or mass insanity
against the horror of life?   What kind of God would create this
thrombotic hostess? About the time one thinks one can make a bit
merry, or enjoy oneself, BAM. . .
as the jaded wonders go on to woo, court, and solicit a rapacity
which has no time for extolling anything which smacks of caring,
around comes the profusive laced in kindness, yak, yak, yaks and I
cancelled the local paper today, the rag about Tammy Faye,

Gary Hart,
negro repression, oyster brained bozos. Don't you ever feel like
screaming?

sometimes a piece of work loses its magic

when it is worked to the point of being sturdy and contrived.

it dies in perfect pentameter

right on the damned platen. the magic starts with a jolt, a

nervous apex, energy,   like a vortex gone mad and then

lies with the planting of stars and laughing

at the monsters who steal time and youth.

the fire rose up and ate the land. it wove itself into blue and yellow

braids licking and belching.   it sent the seeds spitting into the

world and dressed the air in polka dots.

the wind belched,

again in anger and spent itself in great heaves loathing the

fire song and they wed both in anger   both in power

each feeding the other.   the roar went on echoing into the valleys

through the cleavage   and then ran unchecked up and down

the good land, ringed the lakes and spewed out at the water and

the

shores lapped murmuring. The wind laid his breath into the water

and she swelled in adoration,

thrusting giant folds into the wet, the fire sizzled and

spewed again. This time in abomination.

She said you are a nut

Isn't that bizarre   and rolled her head over on the sheet next

to mine

we take lots of time in the sack drilling ourselves about

what could happen wishing it would

but never knowing the future,   just speculating about

what might happen and something always happens

and we never know when it started. It could have started so long ago

but it is so necessary for us to believe that something happened.

The things we do to structure time and fill up

spaces with noise and jabber as if something might happen in the

void

were it not constantly full of this intangible tangible called

something and happen

bibles and bullshit and narratives and all the grande nonsense of life

the children went out in masks.   she didn't wear any.

everyone kept asking her, who are you?   she just smiled.

You don't have a mask.

she just smiled. They would not give her any of their candy. she

would not wear a mask,   she kept banging at their

gates, busy smiling

Is it the little blue men who save you or the little blue men who
destroy you

Coming of Age: You girls,

who milk the light,

turn flint shiney,

pale silk stretched across elastic bones

sex

sabotage your fawn like way through rough age rubble,

slow slipping

into a withered bitterness

as you forgot something you never had . . . breasts billowing

in full naked presence,

firewoman legs ready for the flight into

dark age devoid of soft sounds rising on the hope

of avoiding the sting of   creases cutting flesh

coiling like sinister snakes

sliding their thistly wake down your mid life white sheeted mensa.

. .

gone. . . weeping... letting go, turning light flowing fountains of
milk come rich mother

memories then you girls turning flint shiney

flowering a fleeing fog of fatal femininity

The gargoyles are out plying their off road trails

and tales   and pounding nails into imaginary coffins

.............well, hell, they're all pissed off about Pat Robertson and his

silly nonsense about killing chavez.....................ha, ha, hee, that's a

real kneeslapper, we are funding a war because   sadam

Hussein tried to kill george bushie's daddy. what kind of hypocrisy

is that?   I just love plain old unadulterated stupidity.

even I can spot the gargoyles atop the big spires and spigots on top of

the fountains atop the mountains of lies.

indian summer and the world forgets what time it is . . .

October burns

with bloody colors and you appear at noon to make love to

my armor, the steel thing around my heart with hinges. I am put

together

 with memories, a parcel of stagnant hurt. The green queen. . .

I lick the chestnut odors across your chest and reach for your nipples

stuck up from your carpeted anatomy. My womb curves and beats

as we move sex noises. . .   Dark fantasies and wordless notions

moan. I finish thrashing, the small knot pulsates and is over.

Nerve war.   Cuming.

I have begun to identify with brown bags,

    the unmarked kind.   It's a big deal getting all perfumed

        and made up for the check out lady.

        she has no idea the pleasure she gives me.

her name is Peggy.

that must have been a happy sight, we,

Tara and me   and the delightfully amused old man.

    teachers and me pressed between the cradle and the grave.

        the child became old and he younger than

    when her dimples seemed wrinkles and she said,

"you'd better give your mouth a rest, Mom,"

  and he went right on

smiling

Interruptions are my life.

        I need a ladder to understand this.

I already have a black belt in weirdo.

        Exacerbations. I'm just one big bold bad baby.

Regret: The day breaks   bursting bonnets of benevolence
                         over my broken bowl of buttercup dreams.
You wonder woefully into my maternal moments   and
     steal salt from my solemn soul, silent like a beautiful firefly
you flit in and out of my small silver beacon quiet leaving jet serum
in the pre autumn air where it is not enough I care as you carve
                 and cut until I am like a thin crystal
                        chrysalis ready to break into splintered stars
                 begging for white dwarfed wisdom.
weary winter descends down the long hall and trying tantrums to
overcome   your lack of years
                         like pissing on a playground
             of dirty children and I yowl   about
yesterdays when we were both young and formless little feathers
molting to plates and parody   part woman part child.
where are you when I am trying to reach you in your rubber
     beginnings desperately drawing on your still elastic flesh and
                  impressionable mentality
        someday glad moments moving into being gone
and I will not be there to catch you when you call out my name.
I don't want you to be like me trying to reconstruct a spider's life
long weaving, re-
                 believing I did nothing wrong.

Dollops of disappointment bitter my life

    like autumn leaves dropping too early on the sere

earth floor fading to brown or raked red piles resting before the

wintered altars angle anticipating the cold calamity of snow bitten

mornings whip topped clouds on an azure bloated day. October

dawns

    under sun catching sky wedges geese cutting

 impressions lasting like paper trails on the eternal ether.

never more moments steeped sadder in mute innocence, the world

waxes still born in the bloody sun dancing twilight, disappointment

and bitter blush in the overgrown October banging serenade

wrinkled sounds pelting painful union a gloss agony gore the ice

   evenings as the black marauder steals silent into the rich

    drunken past of lonely once plowed in pleasant

  furrows pregnant with notions of spring eternal

        leaping beyond you,

   October

You cannot kill my spirit,   I know for you have tried,

I saw your need come flooding   before your candor died.

        I do have one more exit

    and I who know all ways,

  would find an exit even made up against the grave.

Sour mud is a let down

weighs a life like all the years spooled

and spent in a tantalizing wait for the peace of knowing

you died drooling a deep drilling dose of anti-happiness

aboard her burning deck

exhuming my long wish to spit bad words

and foul exercises upon the

sour mud thickening cake above

your now impotent flesh

Having recorded the grim reaper's shadow,

I go further out now watching the white caps gather and roll.

Groping, my boat pitches and yawls, moans at me.

I must be careful to not   be caught sideways or upturned.

It's the same in my drunkenness.

The ice chinks in the glass,

that which has become my tower hour after

hour.   It pitches, yawls, moans at me, I must be careful

to not be caught sideways or upturned.

There is no help here in the abyss.

The river has become an ocean all around me licking

my shanks teasing my little bare stripped boat.

There are no answers, silence, just restless sleep,

being careful not to be caught sideways or upturned.

My grandfather is dying,

the last grandfather,

he hears no more, blind, talks like a child.

               Grandfather is dying, the last grandfather,

no one hears my pain, blind pain, hurt, like a child.

Patterns, seasons, time not now,

                    winds that break on profiled stone,

             pitted caverns, wordless tunes, pitch endlessly

against an ancient moon.

My house is full of dust,   My thoughts are naught

  but lust. I'm tired, I sit, I'm full of shit, I'm just a total bust.

They speak of education, the world's a ruination,

                  I wonder why, I just don't die, In

                      pools of urination.

It comes like the tide,

          every few minutes   washing stones and debris

                from a beach made of stone and sand,

        sift, layer upon layer of shells minute, skeletons, sea

castle and promises gone in ebb and flow,

                    eternity of darkness through

      my fault, through my fault, I put your ashes in the kelp and

carry the box away.

        Nothing left but memory, sand castles and the ever

going knowledge,

             repetition, just pain and wash.

The good actress knows

                never to let the tear go

so it sits aborted . . . and abstract just behind the lid

and the poet knows the idea grows   without much explanation

      and the writer grows with

            slow blunted awareness.

I don't got no socks, I don't care, and I don't like underwear.

      Who invented this harness and cotton stocks,

I don't care, I got no socks

Shiva dances and creates the universe,

                              shiva dances, it is enough.

I see shiva dancing. I, behind my blinders, my wagon rumbles

                   the harness runs creases into my flesh.

I must pull on or fly backward into darkness.

       Shiva waxes graceful, astute, melding night into day.

Shiva dances.

I see the stars imploding, dying, shiva smiles, knowing,

      I know too and shiva watches.

      I reach to touch the shadow, pluck it from the midnight,

my hand extends and disappears into the black dancing shiva's

reality.

The wooden wagon thumps, the dark orb is real,

I feel the thick fibers drift through my knowing,

                 soft shiva, hugs my shadow,

pulls me bending into the glass hours.

        Under the purple   mood my pupils skate

spilling liquid prisms.

Shiva holds them, blood arms drawing fingers from porcelain

hooves.

     My womb curves and beats.

              Shiva's non-breath saves me.

Dripping, leaking, weaving salt and weeds through this womb, It is

enough.

Heed well that fine grey friend of busy tail and shifty eye,

    he stores his horde of winter fuel,

        not in the sapling straining more,

        but in the grande tower.

The devious ivy in what seems a gentle lovingness,

        climbs and crawls the strength of trunk,

    on up into the arms and drapes herself in languid beauty,

NOT resting her private, tedious grip.

        Lo, from the sucking, pushing roots,

    the thirsty seedlings battle down, the grub worm fights

     with sticky lips to penetrate the great one's ground.

His arms are bent with birdies' nests and nebulous others

test the bud that spring has spit upon.

        Strength for strength it drills and goes

attracting more the parasitic wise

     until the blood with a shuddered wind is dried.

Easter, Coconut, ecstacy

     emanating organic blood smells. No Christ on a cross, just

jack and me wondering if you'll be home for lunch anytime soon

      after seeing you off to the butcher shop

where they twirled a thing up your groin to your big, sweet heart

and left yellow and purple stains all over past the sides of your underwear.

Then I get you home and we are humble for a week or two
til you lose your temper   and you start in on me with junk
and we throw plates and scream and swell too much. I am sick of
all
your relatives and jealitives and masturbating, self-fixed
fornications all over themselves.

And your former wife, junkie, jackass whore
It's been over thirty years,   now,
                              and I am still seeing that idiot. I
would like to hang upside down on a clothesline with her ass
          sprouting big bags of booga-booga backside barf, or her
twisted relatives roasting marshmallows atop her hideous, fired up
thick head. Hate has a way of turning otherwise civil women into
                              gargoyles or as Mother
used to say succinctly, sinister sisters.
Tonight I will get through the rocks and topography in time
 to wake for a walk with jack and play in the frothy grass, come
home for breakfast tea and toast and hand out medications,
                    do a little laundry and read a few lines of
some favorite book, jot off a thought about how to be more than I
am . . . meow . . .

          misinformed madam of makeup and macaroons,
          coconut dream and conundrums

I'm going to charge you 50 dollars to clean your toilet.

Your carburetor could stand dusting. . .

blow it out on the highway. . . guts in the ether.

Gaseous gluttony.

Everything, including your heart needs oil

I'm so tired of the pubic war,

public conveyances, so and so finds a dead baby on

her asphalt driveway,

George contortion was convicted of being a cum junky.

Check point, caffeine, alcohol, white dust.

Give me another cigarette.

The newspaper kills and social small talk is a lesson in what

lies beneath it all . . . nothing.

So it is I go,

stars and my days,

dancing like a fool and spewing nonsense.

That is the way of the whole human being leaving

filth where there was purity, blindness where there was sight. . . a

moebius of eternity, on and on and on.

Bless the pubic hair at the bottom of my bathtub.

          I loved everyone of them as they grew.

Before they became a nuisance.

     I nurtured their growth much as I have nurtured my own.

I grew and grew. My pubes knew.

       Then I realized how stupid it is

           all this concern for growing things.

I should have known I was alone in all that growth.

               Buried in pubic hair.

Miss m came to class, we needed to get hold of our feelings.

She talked about her strength dealing with her husband's suicide,

affirming all I remember is the bile, vile,

       what did you go and do that to in you trapped,

scratching away at your uniform.

Miss m composed nosed her way back to her seat, deplete, my

basket is full,

     sorrow and one dollar bills.

Where do they put the defogger buttons on these things

and do you mind if we stop for awhile; the heel of my foot

is burning and

     I can't get the blood off my mind.

I fall in love every Tuesday and Thursday

                     at noon when the world is most cruel.

I slip inside your marble cupboard and try to drown in your

undilated pupils.

              They hold me frozen. A statement without

punctuation.

              I am mute amidst the rocks and topography. You

are the master, anchor,

                 your hands reach out and cut the air,

a gesture from a man who knows too much.

                 I listen to your perfect mind and wonder

where the river begins then turn to metaphors and poetry and my

           thoughts are

       caught up in brain doilies,

                flattened inside a plasterboard room.

Falling in love calls me thus, flat, you perfect thing a god has made.

The bizarre in her bra creates unending awe

                 and the wave of her hips is a quake. Her

head has a thing

           like she's shaking a sting, and her lips are forever

gyrating.

For Terry, My Teacher: It was in the art room at the local college
            that my mind first turned to perfect things, visions of
        aspen groves or mountains picking clouds from the sky.
And you taught me a language that embraced silence, a thing we
listened for together.   Your slant eyes came honest
and we bent over ourselves   drawing others
                        into that circumference.
You shudder just West for me, alive
                    or a collage never finished, quite, for
lack of time . . . You with your thoughts about Nevelson and
        O'Keefe   or folded into your movie seat,
            crying and Resurrection.
            I listen to Mahler and dedicate this
        to you as the room breathes me in and out.
            I know a full moon rises over the Sierra, and
you are on the hill, dear friend,
            springing buttercups into existence
            and willing art
                    into all your passages.

Miss Hawthorne went home last night

        retired in a grey bedroom where forty eyes

twinkled in a Christmas ball that hung, bent, from the ceiling.

That is the secret that only Miss Hawthorne knows and children see

sometimes but only when they are alone and very private

my father's last gift to me was a brown paper bag full of some odd

screws, chestnuts, and some sort of tool which I have no idea what

the thing is just that it was handed to me in the bag so lovingly and

spontaneously that we forgot the collection within had no material

worth . . . just heart wishes and soul things, bits of a child's world

broken out of time. I love you, Daddy, and I miss you every day.

That bag has been handled so often that it feels like soft cloth.

I am at once in love with the world and all its creatures. . .

        even the sweet green of the botanical, botanous,

flytrap mentality which will turn on me

        and eat me alive because I am sore and putrid and

just like a flower   in my stupidity.

THE SHIBBOLETH:

Some sit a while asking inaudible questions

      then prey upon the moment painting invisible answers.

Others just stay long enough to teeter on edges

                of syrupy martini glasses; whilst

        in the corner, where light and dust are visiting,

sadness steeps in a mound of decoration.

        How flat it is and counterfeit, this trepidation.

Amid the quips and industry,   I go dressed in indefinity

        and that is all self has ever meant

to crustaceans

This I know,   imagination is often destroyed

by learning; then learning   is a gut level thing

        which can fire the imagination.

It is a double edged sword.

And so we emancipate ourselves from mental slavery,

        freeing our minds, and find ourselves pinned once

more to the inevitable hell   of too much freedom,

      boredom, obnoxious, repulsive, omnipotent arrogance.

The white man is as foul as any race could ever be

as he goes everywhere fouling the air with his stench and waste

and destroying everything in his path.

      Ever his children beget terror as it is in his genes.

        Their way is a great blight

And so it is the monster killer DOES become the monster.

          Still . . . I go about in my blood armor

and cleanse myself thinking I am clean.

        I am old and old and old.

I will die there on the grim reaper's air,

         on his field of doilies just as

the slain brothers before me

      and my little sisters have died birthing.

It is no small wonder that American Manufacturing is being
gobbled up by the Chinese conglomerate, that American Workers
are losing to the hungry Chinese and Indian workers, that our
hospital beds are full of obesity, and that we, as a nation, are losing
our place in the intellectual facilities of the world.

Laziness has taken over the world of prosperity and ignorance reigns supreme with our illustrious leaders who fall asleep while in meetings with Chinese presidents and our president prances up and down in the presence of those who stand down from his wee height.

The Dixie chicks are not proud that george bush is from Texas
.... you know, "don't mess with texas"   I
say, what about

          EARTH   and I'm not a Dixie
Or a chick for that matter.   I'm now a crone and I can't stand what is
Happening in the brown house   with the
ADMINISTRATION..............YOU KNOW, the groupies who live
in the house of
Ill repute   some of them go on these outings where they
Get all oiled up and have no recollection of anything and end up
shooting their friends in the face...........................or themselves
in the foot
they've even adopted a new language for the untied states of the
continent   it's   called
     GUESS WORKER PROGRAM   say what?
What the hell is that? ?   something about texas

The day came and I was asleep

        soft in the cocoon of unconsciousness and then a

something of awareness lit on my soul and I came awake in the

        light of a knowing

today's is LeeAnn's day   big round eyed "oops" it's me she

    might say and titter with a twitter and tiny tee hee

I look for her every time I go there

        where she works and spreads

        Her magic like little cat feet

      even in the heat of a Tucson sunset she

           can be seen with her

"I have a secret smile"   knowing how beautiful she is

  and as she lights with butterfly accuracy on the unawareness

of some blithe spirit coming to see   she   lends

a hope and a kindness in the vast round rink   of possibility

I remember you in your rubber beginnings with your big eyes and

small hands and endless amounts of beauty of telling me

not to cry . . .

        to leave well enough alone.

Getting the run around is the word for the day; shooting accidents occur as the privileged fall into drunkard stupors, and one can only expect lies, lies, lies not only in government but from the loose lovers of gas hogs.

As I become more engaged with the all of everything, I become both more and less important. The tree has both roots and an umbrella. Both serve their purpose and both suck at the universe . . . the roots for nourishment and water, the umbrella for light and air. They work in tandem and lend their wholeness and unique treeness to both the sky and the earth below.

I am an entity of earth and lend myself to the all of things. I hope I am a worthy component.

"INY" is the new media word and the

EMPHATIC exclamation

Lingers

in the air

like a foul smell

flies make strange noises before they die

                they spin and whirr, buzziness on the window still

                they die there like that

                  laid out with their legs stuck up

lost their wings   black or green

      in their segregated cemeteries I kept them in little jars

and their insides evaporated   just legs fell away and a few

whispy, spikey things left.

              Whispers: "wings, wings," sigh

              Such tiny things

reality television is so bad

            we now watch the news to get our laughs

dick cheney shot mr. wittington Sunday last and kept it a secret for

two days.

            He shot him in the face.

I called my best friend from grade school and said, "Rose, I know

          you are a republican

and I forgive you for that; you are still the best friend I have ever

had and I promise I will never shoot you in the face.

        I might talk behind your back.

           but i doubt it.

Some people think love is about charming and high notes

It is also about the ashes and despair

She is my new bookkeeper and she began working the

Minute

she walked in ... very

professional

she worked for three hours then folded her book full of notes and

walked downstairs, looked at

a painting and said, "I make art, too"

pause

"I weave and make baskets both of which require my

math skills"

Then she said, "I wrote 21 poems once.

I just did it"

She left with her notebook and the vision of me with my mouth

Agape.

george bush is now priming us for the biggest secret of all time . . .
it's called the guess worker program . . . even the reporters have
taken up his new lingo . . . what else is on the radar . . . nucular war
with iran, I guess.

i am a tree   rooted

                              and real in my radiance

craving the light ease   my sap runs like blood   and I am

bound

though wrapped in wonder looking upward   I strive

to move beyond that which anchors   me

I got to the airport in Chicago and was waiting at the gate for my

next connection when this rather ruddy looking, overweight, Italian

guy burrowed into the seat next to me. . .

he was carrying what looked like a violin case. I laughed softly and

leaned over and said, "you wouldn't be with the mob?" He said,

"It's a mandolin"

the pollen of my life   the filaments of i

              lay scattered on the floor of earth

                              before the evil eye

be it so   re imagined   my poor body lie

        they would be so happy   were i just born

                                        to die

she spoke of the greater good,

                    pushkin, and dancing with my own essence

          she went on to speak of social order

                          Rudolph Steiner

the individuated person   what are we to be and why

          she said to pay attention to intention

                and went on to address training,

with gentleness and ease   loving

            a field to dance in

she mentioned   aloneness

      and "anyone who does not bring you alive

                is too small for you."

I thought about how it feels to just be   and good

leaving behind my awareness of existential oneness

being

        free and whole and swimming like a seed in the universe

a crescendo of my own, dancing with my own essence and color

        and to quote her phrase: "what I do is me

for that   I came"

Alyson's words at orientation, Spring, 2005

SYNERGISM

i'm dying

again in big gulps while you stand there

in your recycled uniform

look-

I
Ng

important

you'

re just an old b

ag

and your bottom's falling ou

t

you presume to know what will make me well and quote passages

from something

i deciphered while you were out crumbling about

in

such

a hurried worry

                                        yo

                                          u do

the blinking and I'll lay the eggs

                    quietly in my cave by the sea

U

        turn your circles

            and cling to your sick partners loving your

illness

it's just an excuse

                    i will thank you

                            someday

                                    after

i wash away the pain, scabs, torment, humus what

y   ou did in the name of love is

                        e   vil

                    you will pay and

god

                            will

remember

This poem was first written for Alexander Mary with great love and hope

Tiny gifts inspire curiosity like petal pink ones trusted to our arms
We weep with winsome thanks thoughtful of holding too tight tender
Moments having no words small enough to paint our fragile fullness
Poignant pride tiptoeing expressions too big to hold in our hard hands
Wholesome hearts huge idea sated sure we can have one more miracle
She entered a family already full of happy hearts, flower faces bent in awe
Adoration wondering what is this white dream clad in powder smell sleeper
And "here I am butterfly silence" softer than a summer sky simmering deep dressed
Buttermilk fluff or fields of velvet flowers flinging perfume in the dust
She is a mirth-filled moment of child dotted awareness
Laughter lilting like wind upswept, simple, sacheting another kindness given
The way only God can respond to the desire for a reminder of love's long lasting
Pleasure parading through our staccato years halted just so for several seconds
While we ply our skills at creation's way, the secret infinity veil.

I hope she has those big moon orbiting eyes full of whatever "that" is. They are an abyss of beauty. My best love to you all.

this last trip to philly was full of loud sounds and red lips . . . the air

hostess looked like a pagliacci with her big fat butt and red

smacking lips . . . and she had a penchant for ice, I guess as she

used a pick to smash the block of fused cubes . . . Robert frost

would maybe agree as we near the threshold of nuclear war . . .

"some say the world will end in fire some say ice   from

what I've tasted of desire   I hold with those who favor fire. but

if I had to perish twice   I think I know enough of hate

to say that for destruction ice

                                      is also great

and would suffice"

                            robert is resting now and

not to fear the paralyzing ice   not   the

   date we keep with hate.

there was a girl called Monique

whose physique was very unique

she hailed from munich

was found to be a eunuch

and therefore was left out of the clique

you are all the finest I have in my cache of thoughts and pictures of

art pieces I would I were a god of sorts

    all my icons would wear your beautiful face

be   decorated with such as your grace   fine

mind   swept up in the cup of

your   tangible goodness   like your shining eyes,

blue lights in the heavenly stars

when I think of what it must be   to live inside your

mineofgold mind

I try to remember the smell of my mother and the tender moments

of my heart's life

I want to remember about learning to make magic in my tent

away   from

The prying eyes which glare through the fine   mist of

what meaning really is   in life

my life   swift runner   of

               All

                  That

                      The innocent dream

And all that the dear animals   seek   in their

search for sustenance, water

                        Love and care

is breathing still in the soft

    bounty of your hair.

About Susan, my dear friend, June 3, 2006

I knew you in another time   your life was

easy

Your heart was mine

so what is a dangling participle i forget

                              and I also have forgotten what

it is to encounter decency   good manners   well

spoken ladies or gentlemen who are just under the surface,

          naughty   the kind that wait for you in the back

of the cloak room and attempt really pornographic sexual advances

the kind that make a woman giggle in her private parts

                              draw hearts   speak of

mandibles

hannibals   horribles   I don't want my daughter

encountering any of this.

so,   bad as it seems   today is not as bad as the

reporters make it out to be

just it's not like the old days when one waited for hours to smell the

account of death on

the concrete,   terror in

the night

The young woman on the plane was Eastern Indian, she was gorgeous but had bad breath, her eyes were full of smiles and she had gladness in her hints to me when I asked her about the spice turmeric . . . she said to blend it with milk for internal healing and that given with a flour called basin it would rid one of sunburn . . . I don't know but it seemed that was what she said and I don't know how to spell the name of the flour. She said, "it is not like a flower," meaning the word, and I said, "It is like bread flour . . . one syllable" and she nodded understanding with her deep black wonderful eyes. A world of knowledge and kindness passed between us. I gave her my card and my soul went with her.

We were jumping into Tara's SUV and adjusting the car seat straps for the little guys; Tara turned on the engine and the radio was on . . . vivaldi was playing loudly. I reached my hand to the knob to adjust the sound and Riley leaned forward in his seat and said, "just leave dis on, mimi". He's three.

Child one minute, sage the next.

I was getting irritated with the noise level and worried about all the activity so I yelled, "Riley, I am going to clobber you." He looked at me with those huge black eyes and said, "You gonna clobbeu me?" Xander, with his knitted brow and sad eyes, "Don't put Wiwee in de naughty chair, Mom, don't put wiwee in de naughty chair."

We went to see   mother

and fly via st louis to Chicago   on the return

trip   the airport was closed down

so we missed our flight to Chicago which meant we

also missed the connection for our flight on to Tucson

where it is quiet and hot   george bush had the

st louis airport closed so he could fly the air force one jet without

being singled out I suppose   what a supreme idiot.

         No one is going to kill you, george, you are not that

important..........you are just dangerous because you are so damned

stupid and greedy and seedy and pretty much ugly and

vile.....................................while we sat there waitng, a 20 year

old walking blob went by   and several more,

one had a head that looked very much like a loose melon

and his ass was a mash of cellulite probably as a result of all those

hormones the beef, pork, and chicken industries (corporal

corporations) are pumping into the food supply.   Who knows what

is happening to the seeds, the ones used to plant the food like

yellow corn and such, of the world. Why hasn't Michael Moore

written about that? He is an example of the ingesting of all that

junk.   The 20 year old walking blob looked like a

caricature of peter o'toole except for all that fat.   He was

just bobbing along to an unheard song   and I could smell

beef   sort of like a collection center where they

are held prior to going to market. If one drives across this country,

one can smell those places for miles before coming upon them.

They are bleak and nasty, an eyesore on the landscape and you can imagine the smell of fear emanating from the poor bovine bodies and the fright in those large, innocent eyes. The definition of bovine is slow and stupid...

we should definitely change that to describe george bush and dick cheney and their cache of administrative morons......... Americans must be the dumbest people on the planet imagine a leadership of fools...here where cash is king and corporations are the rule and stealing the vote is the word of the day.....................................my mother would have a fit if only she knew.....................................I am glad she has lost her mind.....................................I am losing mine and it started in St. Louis.

it was sunday and there was not much to be happy about or sad

or just weary

the phone rang and it was you   can we make it

over there you asked   the kids

are here with baby quinn and adam and ann and lovely anna

   father joe

Patrick was doing some university thing but they brought the dog

and everyone is having

a bite so I said, "oh, yes" and thought, "that would be lovely. Is

there a better way to

spend a day than in the presence of one so new and uncluttered".

so we went to your house and met the man of the hour, the slant

                blue eyed doll with the

constant smile and gladness fairly burbling out of his every

                pore.................such a baby

        such a gift.................such a perfectly morning kind of

                presence.................and the birds

knew they could not compete with that so they did the conscious

thing and just kept quiet

too bad every being is not as smart as a bird who is in the presence

of a baby prince

                    god probably counted

on that

Aunt Booby and Miss Pussy came to visit and much to our

                        Surprise

Aunt Booby said her   refrigerator was leaking funny

stuff

                   some kind of exotic spice bottles dropping

out of the ice maker but that

was not enough   Miss Pussy was full of wild

reports, as well

                  She said our cereal bowls all had the man in

the moon

showing through   to the outside and

that

                 the bowls had taken up a weird sort of

singing routine   straight up the middle

of the dishwasher

on those rubber coated spikes and began   a

musical howling

               how would you like having spikes stuck up

your ass?

ANTHROPOLOGY

I love these activities   running along beside the

                              Little cart   wondering

where the goat went

Wait   I am the goat
pagliacci   for you

          This vague impelling   pushing me to a

refinement

A tiny vibration   in this pool of chaos and you

speak to me of further

                    Things

The practicing   the words   the moving

                    pieces   there

          On the outside near to where the birds are singing

     one egg kicked

Outside the nest, spilled   like   birth on

the sidewalk

Hermeneutics   interpretation   something
about Aristotle   ontology

                      Phenomenology   reciprocity
  and

Difficult texts   studies in the way of words
     a stream of

              Consciousness

Then right in the middle of your well born narrative, you say to me,
"you have a voice".

              The implications are phenomenal and I am

flabbergasted

The first thing we were told was the business regarding the threat
of west nile virus eating
Into our flesh, carried by giant paradachtile mosquitos craving
blood, raping our veins
And sucking like furious fuckers leaving large red bumps on the
skin   a nodule
or a node from which one would expect   a
monster to emerge
not so the noble   parasitic nerd
intelligent   feeding   fractured
fluke   saved for last   they
came up with more
desert   shit   to gather on the wind
storm not over
the terror play got heavier and heavier   splat
 then came up with the avian   asian   flu
thing   as
if i had nothing to think about   sad
sick   the
doctors wringing their hands   more
experiments on the flesh
                    if there is no water   where will
i go to shit
or drink   or think   or sit like a sumi
on the
brink of   finding out what it's really all about.

this check for $0.14 arrived last july   while

i

                was out selling   a knife or

two

the postage was more than the check   and it

was christopher boehr

vs American express centurion bank, et al.,   superior court of the

state of California

for the county of los angeles, case no. bc256490

checks deposited on or before January 8, 2006 will be cleared, those

after will be void.

I have no idea who boehr settlement administrator is and could not

care less.

Obviously,

what an idiot   we have to dispose of the

envelope and all the

paper

           what kind of business is this   polluting

our environment

in cahoots with american express   what the hell is

the American express

today I went to home depot   i bought a
rosemary plant

                                        and a 50 pound bag of
lime

                                                                what
a crime

the rain was hammering down all around
we were driving
in this direction and the dumb cluck in front of us
had   auto failure

                                        it was terribly
exasperating but we

managed to maneuver our car so as to get past the other gawkers so
we could come on
                        home

we finally got to the light just before our neighborhood and idling
there in a big white

pick up semi   were the license
plates:

Montana   "apportioned"

                        according to what plan?

Bambi is a movie I have seen so many times, he said

                      I have these

                                      kids

you know   he does and he is such a good father
I

wonder if his kids know how excellent he is   always
thinking of them

he's gorgeous, too   and I'm sure the women are
obsessed with him

               his first objective, though, is his kids

he has a girl and a boy and I think an intelligent young woman
would adore him

I can't figure it out   there must be something
wrong with him that I

can't see   maybe he eats crackers in bed or something. I just
can't understand it . . . .and as if that were not enough,

                           he juggles too.

The DEBACLE

What is this   silly non-english phrase mean,
"at de end of de

day"   sounds like some Cleveland plebeian noise

and I cannot understand why in the world andy rooney doesn't
know more about

                              Leonardo and that he is from the town
of vince

Andy says Leonardo painted as an afterthought   how
bout   the fact

That the man was a genius   and just for the
record, andy, he had

Something to do with the anatomy drawings which are still in
medical texts and Gray's

ANATOMY which is a book and has nothing to do with television.
Leonardo would

                              never invent something as base as
that. Probably he was

god's little acre   but one would not expect anyone
here to understand

that with their limited imaginations and stupid conjured up notions
of what are the facts

He did a myriad of things and invented lots of stuff, including the
first air conditioners

which were a lot like swamp
coolers...after all, he lived in

ITALY and was one of the wonderments of the renaissance along
with Michaelangelo

who painted the ceiling of the Sistine Chapel and Titian used to go
down there

and watch him while he worked   they were probably a
pair of the first

known homosexuals

                and I doubt it
had anything to do with how they related to their mothers
just something

they were born to live with   and it was one of those

things they just

had to experience while they painted away their reactions to the

jealousies and

                injustices

inflicted upon them by others   raphael was busy

with the

                school of Athens

and I doubt that he gave a hoot about swear words or tiny wee

minds as he toiled over his

masterpieces . . . his concern depicted there on the left as Plato

transcending the world of

metaphysics and Aristotle on the right illustrating his concern with

philosophy and science

or nature and the interests of man , amazing, that there are still

spoils of indignation

                from dumbos who have

no notion of how incredibly uninformed they are regarding the

upper world and how long

its been steeping in the knowledge that there are those who just

have no clue as to what is

really going on and what is really important, Certainly, it has

                        nothing to do with some

meager attempt by power driven wee folks as they twist their fat,

ugly faces into

                                    contortions of stupidity. It can be seen

on the stations of

television covering the idiotic speeches of george w bush where he

postures and pumps

his shoulders against the air trying to underscore some simple

concept he is incapable of

articulating,   looking at history, one can see we are getting

more and more advanced,

george, and your disciples are certainly a reflection of that.

God will remember what you did in the name of idiocy and he

          will punish your lies and

FABRICATIONS

I wonder if Michaelangelo cared that the stupid pope had him

painted next to the entrance to hell in an effort to impugn his

dignity . . . brilliance is unaware of itself and so much bigger than

that.

mr. rourke: you are filling up my in basket with your unsolicited
mail

 which I find not only a presumptive insult but vastly stupid

and I don't care about your take on anything.. .

you   are not a Cato nor are you Thomas Jefferson.

further, I am not a republican.

I am a registered DEMOCRAT.   I have a brain.

from which part of george bush's anatomy did a foot grow, his
mouth?

        Your statement that george bush is a brilliant orator just
qualified you as an idiot and

        I don't need to hear from another one of those.

oh, no,   you can't go   out
into the rain

                              you'll melt

Ladders are for reaching high spaces

                                            in-between places

                                                    can be

dangerous

if the rung is split

or old

jars can house secrets   words on paper

sweet

                                                        preserves

antiquity   these jars are the stars coming out

                                                        light

in the

darkness and a place for the soul to wonder about

A leather and glass office   smells of contradiction

like a crystal

                                  Gentleman posturing the hours away

in perfect   perpetual   perturbation   trying

with clean hands

to undo an undulating need for

night clothes

and simultaneous naughtiness   while a voyeuristic

virgin squirms in

                            veiled vulgarity.

remembering all   your tiny   new thoughts
that burbled

from your   sweet smelling baby breath
usually early in the

morning   as the years went on
you would resent

my   wanting to preserve those   moments
time

locked   specimens of   love
the time you leaned over from the back seat of the car
after school

                                            at Canton Country

Day   breathing in

                                            excitement

          reporting,   "michelle can't eat attitudes, mom,
attitudes

                              get her all wound up"

or imploringly   at bath time
"when will I get

a hair bottom, mom?"

As a five month old,   sitting in your
grandfather's arms

outside on the spring lawn

you pointed one little fat sugar stick down at the earth and
muttered, "See the bug"

Karen
Horney reported it was really unusual for a child of five months to
speak

intelligently

but it did happen   I know   it
happened

and I also know you described   some pork chops

 we'd had as
rubber meat.
A great testament to my early attempts at being a short order cook.
as a punishment for being out of control

you were made to sit in the Barcelona chair and

listen to

Beethoven's

Ninth

And after listening to the entire piece   we
asked what do you think

of that, Banda   and you said, "It made my heart
dance"

Banda was originally coined from, "Bain du Oiseau" and then
became, simply,

birdbath. . . it was your
childhood nickname

I also remember being admonished and asked simply,
"will you please
coroporate, Mom?"

or your references to blowing up
which meant you had suffered
from extreme
laughter.
Little girls always come up with
the

most extreme names for their   dolls

names like

        "silk"   or "poopoo face"

the pleasure is on the order of a tickling sensation

like

                being a landing strip

for a butterfly.

or having a relationship with a hummingbird

             who will light on your

finger and sit there

I also remember visiting a wild life sanctuary in Australia and after

donning a large bib

        was graced with the opportunity to hold a

baby Koala Bear

and they let me hold him for 40 minutes   afterward

I wept

        and wept   and kept the smell of

eucalyptus leaves in my nostrils

           for a very long time

I suffered Lugubriously after that experience

        and still wonder why it is

impossible

to keep them here on the planet   this planet is too

full of e-viscerated

                              beings to enjoy and respect

something so precious

we had to go through the list of cows . . . brahmas,

longhorn   charolay

white face   angus   Holstein   jersey

Guernsey

it goes on an on   just like a list of

races

                black   yellow   red

white

blue maybe   but they are all cows

      or man   sometimes living in

the same yard

I walk into the rooms and   my thinking

stops   they

Become like devils   posing in haunch

ready to pounce

i become a unicorn   a something magic

can

they tell who i am   i am so beautiful and

innocent I raise

the very devil   who hates me

one and the same

just by being   I have sinned   I have

sinned   bless me

father   for I have sinned

i am at the foot of your bloody windows   light

streams in yellow mucous

color   running   naked color

afraid

i want to lie in the holy water   in the gorey

passion i want to die

through my fault   through my fault

why

has god done this awful thing to me?

it   is   not   important

what are   my

        dreams   only my features

                         still soft

after all the

carnage and bitter wounds   sunsets

leaking into

         daydreams   and sore

esophagal

moments   listing

longing

      wishing for more

           i'm still hungry for

more   more   more

always more

    life   and holding onto   the

things which made

me   me   me

loving so   and hurting in the tomorrows

wanting

the somethings that   made

me so sore

    it is too easy to love a face

It is easy for me to write about being spoken to by a picture, song, or an experience. It seems that everything is an experience to me as I am tactile, emotional, and sometimes I allow myself to experience the world intellectually without the bother of noise, taste, texture, etc. I am mostly contaminated by everything and only god knows what extremes I experience because of my parents, lovers, and siblings. They were all as nuts as I am. I do remember the first time I saw Guernica and was in awe of the way in which the war must have affected Picasso. I set out to try to understand him and found myself in Spain with a bunch of writers, musicians, potters and painters. It was wonderful and I think I came to understand Picasso a great deal. He was very much affected by his passions and the effects of the war were all over him. War is a hideous affliction and suffering is awful though after sixty plus years of living in the world I find that it seems to be necessary for learning to appreciate the life here and how we are molded by our experiences or rendered a dead thing lying alone and feckless, giving up with no hope and no wonder.

Wilma

You were taken away from us by alzheimers disease, an elegant and brilliant woman suddenly in the clutches of a foul enemy who squeezed away the intelligent eyes we all adored, the grand posture, the feminine in our lives which we loved so deeply.

At your funeral, I reeled at the smell of carnations and thought about the fact that I was hurting so deeply because I had loved you so deeply for as long as I could remember. You were already here when I arrived and you had already endured the harshness of your Father's hand and the knowledge that you were not the first in your Mother's heart.

We approached November that year with trepidation and the newness of bitter and sweet, your favorite time of year was now somehow blighted and we were all less innocent in our ways.

I remember the story of Ruth from the Bible and wondered at the impact it must have made on you as you recounted the telling of it to me when I was a middle aged woman. Oh, how I wish I could tell you how very important you were to me as we approach the December Holy Days and hear about war and greed, kidnapping and starvation.

And so I determine to pay greater attention to simple things like habits and home baked bread and I vow to love my friends a little more and pay less attention to their barbs which are born of jealousy and more respect to their acts of love and kindness.

I am recently finding my slow growing blunted awareness is changing, probably because I have encountered the grim reaper so often in my life and the latest episode bleeds a little deeper into my life.

When I lost my husband to suicide, I had great periods of time missing so I did not remember the horror but I do remember the pain, like labor, it came in waves and I was so engulfed in it at those moments that I don't even remember being here.

I love those persons who look at me with mounds of selfness in their souls and talk to me about being upbeat and positive and how God has plans for me. Who among us knows what God knows. Those are the people who spread the word that life is about the charming and the high notes; it is. Life is also about the ashes and despair.

I remember the sweet smell of my grandmother's garden and the first taste of a green apple. I remember boiling jars after the washing ritual for canning season and the making of narrow, straight rows for planting corn and beans, peas and radishes. I also dream of the boiling sky before an Ohio thunderstorm and the smell of ozone afterward or the earthworms coiling the ground.

Mother used to line a clean cardboard box with waxed paper and pour hot, lye soap in it to set up and then cut with grandmother's old butcher knife. I remember the smell of the soap and watching Mother cut it into shavings over the washing machine tub as it melted into the steaming water and the glorious odor of the clothes and sheets as they were taken from the line. The line was propped into the wind by long pieces of wood which were notched to hold the rope lines into the wind. In winter, that was an arduous task.

Mother used to say, "the beautiful and lovely have their place in life, but it's a fragile place and the first thing to go when disaster strikes". I am sure that was a sentence some famous person said but I don't remember who it was . My Mother was full of wise thoughts and sayings and as her Father said of her, "Glanna was smart but Wilma has always possessed depth". He just said, "she was deep".

I wonder how deep the hurt must go to see your first born slip swiftly into the ashes and I wonder about the despair and the agony . . . it was the first thing you would remember as you remember being a girl come into your season and then losing your tiny baby sister who died just as you were sixteen and she was only three. You followed the death of your first sister and because of her death, you were a resentment my grandmother stroked over and over and passed on to your own babies.

Today I left my house at 6:45 am to get to my new art class; I was fully awake knowing I had to walk up several flights of stairs carrying a heavy load and then return to my automobile to fetch more of the supplies needed. probably I would be making three trips in order to get it all there and then I had to be a nice person and deliver the extra stuff I had purchased for the other two females at my table . . . they are probably about 21 and I am 62 with a gimpy leg and other problems . . . probably why I'm 62 and still trying . . . well, I don't know why I bothered going at all. Yesterday, while we were finding out what the class is all about, another crone, skinny, ugly, and way too pushy, came up to the back of my chair and being the bitch she is, starting bushing and invading my space at which point I said, "do you mind?" her retort, "why don't you go live in a ping pong ball" . . . I left class with that attitude and went off to the various stores assigned to gather my needed supplies and those for the other two younger girls. After doing those chores, we went on to the motor vehicle department to have our Mercedes checked at the emissions control stand. A corpulent, sweating, male pushed down on the gas cap and broke it. I was told by a female supervisor that he was one of the best inspectors they had and had been there a long time . . . he looked to me to be about 20 years old. Anyway, we went off to the Mercedes dealership to get a new gas cap. the Mercedes dealership service department gave us a pink slip and told us the task had been accomplished so we went back to the MVD to carry on with the proceedings . . . we arrived only to be told that the cap would not work properly at which time we ascertained that the cap, had, in fact, not been changed so we went back to Mercedes for the second time and got into an altercation.

We were admonished for losing our tempers and left after being
given a new gas cap . . . we just went home to tackle the problem
the next day . . . I went on to a medical appointment to be told that
my bladder or kidneys would need to be inspected for possible
complications such as stones or cancer or maybe nothing as I recently
had an episode with a lot of blood in my urine while on vacation
visitng my sister and her physician saw me, gave me some high-
powered antibiotics, and told me to see my regular physician after two
weeks had expired so I did that and made the necessary appointments
for a Urologist, and so on, at which time the phone rang and the
Arizona department of the internal revenue service was giving me
a call to tell me I owed $18.05 in back taxes and would I put a check
in the mail ASAP to cover that and so I performed that task and
was getting ready to do something else when the phone rang and
the doctor's office was calling to inform me that my urine was
missing in action and could I come back and give them another one.
At 4:00pm I collected the mail and found another letter from the
California branch of the IRS telling me that that we owed $9000
......................what the hell do I need a job for anyway...all I do is
correct the bullshit that perpetually clutters my life. I will go have
the urologist, et al, inspect my physical status and pay the bill
which my insurance will not fully pay even though the charge me
nearly $1000 a month because I have poor records due to a stroke I
experienced while under the care of a male who was posing as a
physician and was actually a male nurse. At the time of that fiasco,
we were living in an area which had long been forgotten by
intelligent people and was inhabited by gargoyles and assholes.

are american postage stamps made in china

i purchased a roll of postage stamps and couldn't open them
without using the medal on my key and then I had to stand there
trying to figure out how to unravel the tape which came off in
pieces while it also desecrated one of the stamps the age of
simplicity is certainly gone with the dissemination of all that holds
any sense in the American societal hodgepodge now I am crazy on
a minute by minute basis as the cost of fuel skyrockets and
the ease of eating just about anything wholesome is ruined for me
because I learned about what is really going on and the thought of
wearing a pair of leather shoes is totally disgusting because now I
can't even bear the thought of what happens to animals and how
they give up their lives so I can parade around in something of a
dyed hide and feel pride in being well dressed and pressed what a
mess finding out how disgusting I am for being a human who holds
no regard for other beings or the beautiful splendor of the
grande earth orb suspended on such a tedious place run by the foul
likes of politico the dictionary I have owned for 40 years doesn't
serve me anymore as the language is so totally different now that
the dictionary hasn't even got the new world words in it and I have
to find out what is modernity and late modernity and post
modernity and globalization so I can try and ferret my way through
what was already a complicated passage no thought of those who
grew up in an earlier time and its no wonder my mother and father
shook their heads in desperation not understanding what was

going on when I was just trying to explain the importance of
accepting those who had a different sexual bent oh, it's gone far
beyond that it seems as huge corporations are now considered
economies and there are more of them than land mass
individuations and they are changing the world of nature
engineering genes and killing of species with their pollution and
possessions just when I thought I had arrived where being a girl
was going to be a place of clear point acceptance without the fear of
subjugation or reading about places where a girl's clitoris is cut out
in a tent by men while she screams in agony and reduction how can
I put this down in such a way that it will be read in
understanding and hope there will be a reverence for the mother
who holds her son in pride and is respected for seeing to the
rearing of that child and the warmth of the hut or that she put some
food down for the sustenance of the family I am trying to get over
sobbing and learning that learning is an obstacle course which
requires persons to abdicate feeling and just accept the fact that the
world is no longer about anything as simple as expecting to buy a
roll of postage stamps and understand that they will work

It is said   in the mayan history passed on

and on through

pie holes   that

                                                           the

world will wobble

on its axis and end somehow   on December 12, 2012

being here is so much fun   i remember

from the time

                    i arrived being told all the horrors

   of not living up   being

damned to hell

                    looking forward to the killing,

chilling out in a cold grave   it's so fun

and now

                    i am looking forward to the end

          wobbling   the horror

being

     thrown into oblivion   or

meeting death

                    somewhere out there

                                    on a pale horse amid

the stars and

great stones   a monolith in the

ether

          a mayan myth on a mission

who is this blonde, brittle, boney bitch
ann coulter?

She is described as being a constitutional lawyer
What the hell is a constitutional lawyer?
I know that corporations are entities I always
thought the constitution

Was a brilliant body of work by a boat load
Of brilliant men Alexander Hamilton
John Jay

James Madison Benjamin Franklin et al
when her SHRILL accusations come
echoing

through my family room at the television hour, I
WANT TO RUN
COVER MY EARS AND AM IMPUGNED
wondering

Who in the world let forth that angled
attorney We already have enough of those
it would be nice if women began to think of themselves as
respectable societal pillars upon whom the world of importance is
cemented, consecrated, defined..................

Women can be intellectually glorious and with the bright
influence of years

steeped In intuition
definitely a gaia kind of thing a god
consciousness
Who in the world wants to be a man? I don't.

Men plan it all for us

economies   corporations   corpuscle

muscle

corpulent   fat heads

            I want to scream   how I have

come to hate

     Man   bawling and beating his chest

He created god in his own image   like the dim light of

the KKK fires

Same kind of idiocy   white this time but

very much like

          Muslim   islam

Chicken bastards hiding behind their shrouds   like

women hunkering behind

       burkas   unevolved

theocrats

       Dressed in black to signify strength and secrecy

it's no secret

evil screams in its

           need for being noticed

jumping up and down in the streets   making noices like

infants needing a spanking

you have the audacity   but I have the intelligence

you have your

      guns

        i have my mind

who's gonna win that one   we'll see.

Her nefarious fingers fiddled   with the

hung photos dangling

from   book shelves   just as her jugular jars

filled   like some

     pregnant   prehistoric

paradactyle

     a metaphysical memory morphed onto her computer

cone

parallel planes pulsed   a parabolic piece

of possibility and

     her cranial file   difficulty

ERASED

 cosmic   contradiction   inflicted space

between

     the omaan and the oracle

subsidizing   salacious sycophancy

which habituates in

Washington, dc   amid the saturated

supercilious

ego ridden radicals   amalgamated,
propagated

convenienced   conflicted little minds
gathering guts

for great glorious   poo poo faced evil bred
boneheads

                                        clad

and celled

 like black heads   in puss ridden
hell holes

It was humus first   before it seeped liquid into

the ball of earth

                                                                                compressed

compounded

running a dark,   mysterious   fluid

river

                                                                        spouting

middle east   gold

smelly   then compacted more from

bituminous to

anthracite   black   coal to

coke

                                furnaces for corporate fuel   and

left   untouched

                                                                                        becomes

harder still   shining like the shrill

bitch

who wears it   posed   on   her

white finger

I met her as she hurried by at the Gourmet Products Show

and I don't recall if it was Javitz or Moscone   but we

were impressed with the urgency with which

She   talked   red hair   and   that air   given

to people of intelligence   and presence…………………….

We love you, Connie   more than you could understand as

we are out of hand   and   far away

we know it might be our turn   next and we might

need to display

some   or a   little   humility   like you

pressure under fire   the fire of living   with the knowledge

we are all here for just a little   time   hope we can pass on

dignity   have a bit of integrity   your display of grit

          Has made me oh so humble

My darling girl   I hope you know   I am full up

Of hurt for you and I hope you don't let it get you this

other time   so many times

                    Love   myra

The first time Riley came with his daddy

he spent 24 hours his brother stayed at home with mom

we had lots of fun though he was only two and he was drinking

sprite like a hot man with a cold beer………………….he'd just put it to

his lips, sling

his head back and drink and then he'd go ahh.

i sit here counting hours now that I'm 62 and wonder where all the

time went while I was getting on to being old   past,

actually   as I wrestle with

Hypertension   giving in   burning from shingles

and wondering

if we'll have a pandemic   or nuclear war

the red spots sting

why don't they itch   would I be better off dead

you are unconcerned with vanity   as you pat your thinning hair

most of it has already fallen out

and I think my eyes are going so

you tell me not to worry   they can replace my old lenses

                    then you cast a string of words my way

the kind that smack of poetic syntax   the meaning stings a

little as I am still not at the point

where I have forgotten what you said   but I let my

mind wonder just a little   to seeing paintings in my head

the moment evaporates like transparent people   and

words atomize   in the thick

Toxic vapor   dense fog where the fat people

wiggle around

I listen as you become the artist there   your hands like

fragile fans

dipping and weaving meaning through your monologue

            an aura arrives slowly around your

thin body   then I know I have switched

so I zero in on those   two tiny pupils you've aimed my way

mean like thinking   I'm just another meaningless piece of

furniture   and

As they become harder and imploded   they seem to

rise up and boil

When we were young I would just become extinct or petrified

sitting with definition

bound, dense, cold   like marble

deaf in your un dilated   egomania

sucking me up

grinding me into the dust   counting   just counting

now that I sit   just sit   aware of the time

as it ticks off into   eternity

Short Stories

The Rejoinder

It was nearly time for the funeral. John sat holding the register. Outside, the leaves were turning, falling, sifting gold onto the sidewalk. Inside, the smell of carnations permeated everything. The hallway reeked of them. Something else scented the air in the foyer, smelling of bruised hyacinths and cake icing . . . sweet.

John stared, unblinkingly, through the clear, glass windows. Three of Lynn's poet friends were coming up the walk, heads bowed, talking. The trees rustled and belched, sending a stream of leaves, a fire-vision, to jig along over the sere earth carpet. Framed in the window amid the leaves and color, the trio grew as they came closer.

"They aren't talking," John whispered. "They are each writing a poem . . . another page in their collection." He closed the register, stood, and walked over to the stand. He laid the book down, unopened, and left the room.

Walking down the hall, John met little Maria. She ran to him, her arms outstretched.

"Oh, Daddy," she laughed, "don't be sad; come with me. I will show you the baby dinosaurs. Two of them are playing ping pong in the refrigerator."

"Don't, Maria. Not now. There is no refrigerator here."

Her little body straightened. "Oh, yes, Daddy, but there is. Come on. I will show you."

John held her tiny body away from his; her soft arms were fragile in his grip. He looked into the big black eyes. They were soft. Blue pockets lay under them.

"Maria, your mother is being buried today." John looked down into the carpet. He thought of Lynn, lying silent in the next room. He swallowed hard. "Maria, this is not the time to play imaginary games."

She blinked. "Yes, Daddy, I know. I promised Mama I would help. She asked me to help, Daddy." The little face distorted slightly. "Oh, Daddy, let me help." The small hand reached up and patted his face. John felt like someone were bathing his face in warm water. "It's all right, Daddy, I'm here."

"Where is nurse?"

"She's in the room over there, Daddy. She has baby Marvin in the pram."

John stood. He plugged his feet into the carpet, extended his hand to Maria, tugged, and launched himself off down the hall. The child jogged along beside him.

He peered down into the pram. The pink infant lay sleeping in the pram beside the brown mahogany end table. A clear candy dish sat on the table, full of shiny, pastel-colored jellybeans. Maria stuck her fist into the dish. The jellybeans rattled. The infant opened its swollen, pink mouth and squealed.

"Oh, Maria, you've disturbed Marvin. Where is nurse?" John turned, striding out into the hall. Maria followed. Her white dress flipped around her small legs. Her knees twinkled as she ran along in her shiny, black-patent shoes.

"Wait, Daddy, wait for me. I'm right behind you." She tripped on the rug and fell. John turned. She lay quiet, the air gone from her. Finally, she looked up at him. Her eyelids fluttered, trying to hold the tears. "I'm Ok, Daddy, it doesn't hurt me."

John trembled. He was suddenly touched by the small child's understanding, her desire to be brave.

"Maria, please be careful. You will spoil your dress."

"Yes," she picked herself up. "Yes, I know, Mama bought it for my party."

"Well, we'll go back into the room with Marvin and wait."
The baby was wailing, batting the air with two spastic fists, his face exploding into a pink misery. Maria shoved another jellybean into her mouth.
"Maria," John scolded above the baby's cries, "why are you eating all that candy? Where did it come from?"

She lowered her eyes at him. "They were for my party. Too late, though, no party." She laid a pink one on her tongue. John looked at her, unable to say anymore. Finally, he bent over the baby's pram and lifted the small bundle out. He rocked Marvin to and fro. The baby quieted and began to hiccup. The nurse entered the room.

"I'll take him, John." The nurse spoke in a clipped, terse manner. "Maria," she continued, "that's about enough candy. Go wash your hands, now, and we'll remove your pinafore." Maria whimpered. She covered the pink stains with her little hands.

"No, it's my party dress. I'm wearing it for Mama. NO," she yelled loudly, "I won't take off my pinafore."

"She can't separate it, Nurse. Just let her alone." John picked up Maria. "It's all right, Maria, you may keep your pinafore."

Nurse gave John a stern look. "Leave her to me, John, and don't fret."

John went through the door and walked back down the hall. The three poets were huddled together around the register. They seemed to be swaying into each other, gesturing, plucking the air and bending. They saw John in a simultaneous instant. They ceased moving and became stiff, expectant.

"I expect they think I should address them in 'free verse'," he thought, remembering all those poetry reading sessions, the stages, the spotlights, the poets posing as fragile bouquets, vased against the night. A cynical smile had laid itself across his soul. "Hello, you three," he said at last. "Should I say how glad I am you came?"

For one long moment it seemed as though the four of them were suspended, unable to move, frozen into an ice-globe. John's mind worked. "Don't be sarcastic. Don't be cruel." He thought about the last lines of Lynn's twilight poem,
Not for you embracing,

My need still crawls, racing,

And the inability to live.

His eyes were accusing.

"John," Francis began, "we didn't know what she meant to do. We had no idea."

"No, of course not," James finished. His British accent lifted the words.

"If we had, don't you think we would have told you?" Timothy offered.

John stared at them, not feeling. Words from James's poem about death and Americans punched through John's mind. He replied, "No, I don't think you would have told me. I think it all appeals to your morbid sense of aesthetics. You are all so ingrown and malignant. You pitch from one bizarre, ugly, human event to the next, taking notes all the while."

Francis sucked in air. "My God, John."

James started to open his mouth. John swung around to meet their eyes. Pain washed through his limbs. He was shot through with adrenaline.

His voice began in a horrible whisper and rose louder and louder. "Don't say anything now, James. Don't say anything that sounds right. Save your thoughts for later. You should have brought along a tape recorder." John's face was wet. His mouth pulled into a grimace. Blood pumped through his words in an orgasm of grief. "We all know how people don't die in America."

"John," Francis whispered.

"Shut-up, Francis. Why are you here, anyway? Why did you come? So you can weep? You need to weep."

Francis shook her head, "we loved her too, John."

"Yeah," John said, throwing the word at their bodies. His voice jerked forth in a hideously restrained hatred. "Yeah, you loved her. You understand, don't you? You understood all the time. Well, she's here for you, posed there on her death pillow. The grim reaper came at last. She is sheathed now in perfect pentameter." He turned a violent half circle and stopped. Approaching the casket room, he muttered, "and I was the odd man out."

There was a pink blur. The brown box grabbed his eye sockets. He walked into the perfume and reeled. Still he walked. He reached out to touch the small form and recoiled. Her soft skin did not move in the pink dress. There was only the scent of carnations moving through him, filling him. Pink glowed on his arm. A pain banked in his gut. Nausea gripped him.

Aloud, he said, "you have left me with our poetic progeny. Two pink gifts that wax important." He thrust his hands into his pockets, his eyes closed down. He talked, "yes, pink. Pink like you. A gift? Pink things always are." His hands moved into the seams of his pockets. A small, round thing lay at the bottom of the pocket. "A jelly bean," he muttered. He raised it up, letting it roll into his palm. It had already lost its luster from the heat of his hands. He pitched it into the cluster of pink flowers. A petal flapped, the flower nodded. The orange jellybean fell under the blur . . . alone, sticky, on the carpet.

The Parcel

She sat quietly on the oak chair in the kitchen. There were six of the chairs lined up against the stuccoed wall. The smell of hemp drifted through the room and mingled with the scent of oregano and paella. A long, dark, wooden table stretched the length of the room. On the far corner of the table there was a pile of bright yellow lemons and an empty pitcher. Mitka's eyes were alive with appreciation. "This room," she thought, "is like a painting."

She listened to the muffled conversation in the room behind the tapestry curtain. Every minute or so, the voices would rise and fall off into a mumble. The words bumped into the walls and echoed out into the kitchen. Now and then, the stronger voice would rise in agitation and Mitka would catch a word. The harshness of that one voice frightened her. She felt she were waiting for an interview or an astounding event of grave proportions. "What am I doing here? When I tell him why I have come, he will laugh at me . . . maybe he will be angry." The heat and the wind were beginning to annoy her. She began to sweat.

Finally, the curtain was thrust aside and a small dainty male dashed out. He quickly excused himself and sped through the door. His face was scarlet and there was a terrified look in his youthful eyes. Mitka watched his exit, her mouth slightly open. She saw the dust boil up behind him as he darted down the path toward the sea.

She turned and jumped. The man stood there looking down at her. His arms hung loosely at his sides, and his beard seemed to wave against the oppressive heat. "Yes," he said, "and you must be Mitka. I've been waiting for you all morning." The wind wailed, long and low. Mitka sat staring up at the thick, cotton-clad figure. Strength radiated from beneath the white collar. His neck was a warm pink. His eyes were indigo blue and pierced her own. Her eyes stung from the intensity of his.

"You were waiting for me?" She asked disbelievingly. "I am surprised you know my name."

He walked over to the lemons on the tabled and stood there for a moment, eyeing them. Then, with deliberation, he reached out and picked up the fattest, most perfect one from the pile. With his big hand, he began to knead the lemon, gently. "Yes, well, I know everything that goes on around here. I know who comes and goes . . . names, faces, backgrounds." He was slicing the lemons now and squeezing the juice into the pitcher. "This is my village, my island, my world." He paused and looked into Mitka's eyes, then he let his eyes wonder the length of her young body, taking in the curve of her waist and her long, tawny legs. Mitka blushed.

"I would like to hear about the legend." Mitka blurted the words out as if she were spitting something distasteful from her mouth.

He poured water into the pitcher, "will you have some cool lemonade with me? I've taken the seeds out." He filled a glass and stirred it with one big finger.

"Funny," she thought, "I expected him to be frail and slight with square hands."

He offered her the glass. "Have you a manuscript or a poem? Young writers have so much to say, so many words." Mitka blushed again. She thought, "He must be reading my mind." She stammered, "Oh, no, I have nothing for you . . . nothing to read. I haven't anything. I just wanted to hear about the legend."

"The legend. You mean the giant who sleeps in the mountains." The wind rushed hard against the walls.

"The giant," she thought, "or the wolf, what does it matter. Just talk, damn it." Mitka's impatience made dimples around her mouth. She watched as he poured himself a glass of lemonade.

"You are the giant, aren't you?" The question startled them both.

"All these young writers come here because they are in love with you." Mitka bit her lip. The wind heaved again, mockingly, and a great amount of sand spit through the crack under the door. She drank and flinched. Her lip was split and the lemonade stung.

He turned and walked closer. He stood over her again. "The Sirocco has been blowing for seven days now, have you noticed?"
"Yes," she addressed her sandals, "I can't keep a candle lit in the evenings. I wish it would stop."

He smiled and took a long drink. "No one can leave when the weather is like this. There is a lid over us. The wind won't let the clouds move. It flattens them down over the mountain and seals us here."

"What are you getting at?" Mitka was becoming uncomfortable.

"That's how the legend started . . . with a Sirocco. It blows up the coast from Africa carrying sand and debris. I think the myth was carried here the same way." He chuckled and lowered his big frame into the chair next to Mitka's.

She smiled at him though she didn't find his comment humorous. "I think it's strange," she said, "The wind, I mean, and the villagers. They behave so odd since the wind came. Maybe it's because they're confined and can't be swimming and visiting on the beach."

"Well," he began, "the legend is a product of the wind and superstition . . . the Majorcan mindset. A person isn't safe out there when the Sirocco comes because of the sand and the heat. People get a little crazy and wander off into the wind. Sometimes they are lost and die out there . . . in the mountains. No one ever seems to find the bodies, true, but I've never known anyone to really try."

"You mean they just leave them out there like that?" Mitka was astonished.

"You must understand how primitive some of these people are, Mitka." There was irritation in his voice. "When a whole people believe in that sort of magic and have gone on believing for ages . . ." His voice trailed off and he sighed. "I wonder sometimes myself if the giant is real. I can feel him here." He looked around at the walls and then he laid a hand on Mitka's small shoulder. "We will go into my study shortly, and I will show you where I work. Would like to see where I write? I sleep in there, too."

Mitka uncrossed her legs and deliberately turned her big eyes on him. A strand of hair fell across her eyes. He reached up a hand and scooped the hair from her face. She looked down. The intimacy embarrassed her. "This great man is petting me," she thought, "If I move, he'll eat me." The thought sent her into a fit of nervous laughter. He was startled and reared back with a comic look on his face.

"Your reaction to affection is interesting," he said, "would you like some more lemonade? I am going to have some more." He rose from his seat and walked over to the pitcher.

Mitka had recovered her composure and was feeling ashamed. With her eyes cast downward, she said in a small voice, "Yes, I do; I would, I mean." The room was silent except for the sound of lemonade pouring into the glasses. The sound was big in the silence.

"I, I like copper," Mitka tried again.

"I like it, too," he replied, "it gleams when it is polished. Under all that tarnish, there is a gleaming, rich intensity. Copper tarnishes quickly, even when it's new." He handed the glass to her. She drank then raised her hand timidly and wiped the pulp off her lip.

"I thought you would refresh yourself with something more sophisticated than lemonade."

"Like what?" He questioned, amused.

"Oh, something like Scotch or Bourbon . . . whiskey."

He snorted, "How do you think I write? You've read too many accounts of the lives of broken writers who have fallen into a pit. That's not romantic or interesting, or glamorous, that's just silly. My life is very simple, elegant, I think, like those pots and the lemonade."

Mitka felt his eyes burning her. He sat down again on a farther chair. "Do you think the giant will get me?" She giggled and drank the last of her lemonade. She let the pulp rest of the tip of her tongue. It was tart and stung a little. "It reminds me of brine," she said aloud . . . "something just a little harsh in its innocence."

He laid his eyes on her for a long moment letting her words settle over him. "No, Mitka, the giant will not harm you. The giant wants to protect you and keep you here amidst the goats and the knotted legs of the olive trees, the abundantly full lemon trees." He looked down at the glass in his hand. An empty moment followed. "The giant belongs to this place, the people, and the African winds . . . and those big yellow moons." There was a silence again. "The giant will never hurt you."

Mitka was moved by the longing she felt rushing out of the big man. He was old and lost for a moment.

"You belong to the morning. The giant celebrates the morning. It's when he rests."

She felt fragile and tired and an intense need to leave the confines of the house came over her. She rose, "I should go now."

"Oh, he replied sleepily, "well, I won't detain you." His manner was formal, now, guarded. "I don't talk about the legend with anyone. You knew that, didn't you?" His voice was accusing.

"Yes," she said, "I knew. I'm sorry. I didn't realize . . ."

"No," he stopped her, "Not to be sorry." He reached out for her hand. "It's not often I dance with a perfect turning lady."

"May I come again?"

"Yes, perhaps the next time we'll be more comfortable," he said slowly.

"Yes," she repeated, "Yes, and you have touched me."

She turned to go, her long arms swinging freely. Her blue dress caught in the wind, fluttered teasingly around her legs. A line from a verse trolled through her head and began a monotonous rhythm: *And if he then should dare to think of the fewness, muchness, rareness, greatness of this endless only precious world in which he says he lives – he then unties the string.

*From: A Warning To The Children, a poem by Robert Graves

Stage Business

The recording studio was hot, scorching Kathryn's neck. The yellow lights drilled down as she bent over the microphone. Slowly, she began a rocking motion. Her hands knotted. Again and again her fingers moved out from her fists. Her appendages, like sea anemone shifting in violent undercurrents, danced a primitive rhythm. Her mouth moved on and on. Her voice climbed, accelerated, and nearly died away in her plea, "please, Daddy, please. Oh, please, Daddy, give me back my doll?" The tape session ended. Kathryn sat. A salty wetness permeated her clothing as though each of her cells were seeping. "Good God, I feel as though this madness were claiming me." She stood. Laying the back of her hand to her forehead in a wiping motion, she muttered, "I've never experienced such fear in a script . . . this business of being crazy . . ." The door of the studio flew open and Michael strode into the little room.

"Really, Kathryn, darling, you were marvelous! Go get a drink?" With a dry mouth he quickly stamped her wet cheek. "This is hard for you this time, isn't it?" He bowed, thrusting his head down between his knees in an absurd gesture. "Our poor, dear Kasey is tired. Let me buy the lady a drink? The weather isn't so bad tonight. Maybe you would like to walk? Oh no, I think I would rather see you home in the car." Not waiting for a response, he chattered on. Quietly aware of his monologue, Kathryn busily collected her things.

"I've never known anyone with a greater gift for pushing air around. Why does he flog around that way?" Kathryn smiled, "so tired," she thought. "I am a strong scented plant with bitter leaves."

"Ready now, Kasey?"

"Yes, I'm ready, Michael, and you know I welcome these late night sojourns with you."

"Uh-huh. That's because you don't have to pay any attention to me. Gives you time for your own mental business . . . living in your head."

From the corner of her eye, Kathryn looked at Michael. "That's because you never say anything worth listening to, Michael." Reaching over she squeezed his hand affectionately.

The car was cool. Carried away by the lull of the motor and Michael's voice, letting herself sink into the seat, Kathryn stared out at the night. It occurred to her that Michael was saying something important, "said she was known for some time now. If you know what I mean. Their relationship looked quite hot."

"Who?" Kathryn asked, "Michael, what in the blazes are you talking about?"

"Oh," he responded, "See, you should listen to me more often, darling. I'm really wonderfully interesting, don't you think? Why, my mind fairly teems with mediocrity and obscenity . . ."

"Don't Michael, you know I appreciate your attention. But never ending babble, I can't stay with you in that."

"Well, maybe it's best, anyway, dear Kasey. I seem to have a bad case of the hot nasties, if you know what I mean."

"No, I don't know what you mean. And what's all this hot business, Michael? Will you please tell me what you are talking about?"

"Oh, a little gossip I picked up about your old man . . . way out here, too. Isn't that rich?"

Fear beginning to percolate in her head, Kathryn felt her body contract. Slowly it began to crawl through her limbs, heightening, gripping her, now faster as though it were beating its way through her body to the outside, her heart pounded. "This is crazy, Michael, but I have to have some air. Please pull over."

Jerking around for a quick look at her, Michael slowed and cut onto the shoulder of the road. The car bumped to a stop. "What's the bloody problem, Kasey? Hey? I didn't mean to upset you. Holy God, I'm sorry. You look awful, chum. Are you ill? What can I do Kasey? Can I help?" He stopped talking.

Kathryn started to say something and he interrupted. "Ah, I know what we'll do. We'll go to that little place up the road here and have a cup of hot chocolate. That's what you're after, a little something sweet to cheer you up. Heavens, darling, you really gave me a start!" Michael pulled back onto the road. His hair was mussed from all his gesturing at Kathryn. He had a frantic, pathetic look. He kept looking over at her appealingly.

"Quit being guilty, Michael, I'm just imploding for the moment. You know how I hate my father."

"Yes." Michael sat in silence.

"Ok, Michael, you started it. Let's hear the rest."

"It's nothing, Kasey, really, it's nothing."

"Michael?"

"I met this broad a party the other night. She said she knew about my show from the radio tapes and that she was with your old man."

Kathryn spoke into the windshield, "And?"

"He was there, Kasey, I met him."

"Well?" She said loudly, "And what did you think of him?"

"I don't know," Michael began slowly, "I thought the chap a bit oily. Something strange about him. He was quiet and small, rather doll like, if you know what I mean." He went on thoughtfully, "He seemed much larger, though, you know . . . dreadful or something."

"Yes, I know," Kathryn retorted. Silently, she reflected, "Doll, give me back my doll, indeed. How extraordinary." Silence filled the sedan. "Michael, please, if you don't mind, I'd like to go home. No chocolate, thanks."

"You're sure?"

"Yes, quite sure. And Michael, I'm not angry with you."

Kathryn lay on her bed staring at the insects inside the glass-domed light cover. "Bugs," she whispered, "we're just like bugs. We flit and flirt with life and it blinds us. When we are sightless, we just give up and tremble a while." She turned her face into the bed. Pulling the pillow over her head, she groaned, "all those years, those awful years . . . what is it? Something about dolls?" She flipped over fast, slapping her body against the mattress. Her eyes glistened with a knowing look as she glared into the light fixture. "Yes, something about dolls." She looked away, the light echoing in her vision. A doll's face flashed in a strobe effect. She tore at her hairline and shook her head, "Go to sleep, Kasey, go to sleep."

"Tomorrow came, didn't it?" Kathryn broke the eggs over the skillet, one two, three. "Three?" A crooked smile creased her face, "Good heavens, get hold of yourself, girl." She flipped the tuner to a classical music station. "What I need now is The New World Symphony." Hurriedly, Kathryn slid the eggs onto a plate and sat down dutifully. She greeted them cautiously and smelling the odor only exuded by eggs, she reflected, "I can't eat these things, they're looking at me." She slipped out of the chair and went into the bedroom to dress for work.

Michael sat behind the desk with the blunt end of a pen stuck in his mouth. He kept sucking at it, rolling it around, pulling it out, then pushing it in. "Michael, for God's sake, stop that infernal fixation. Sometimes I can't stand you." She gave him a bold stare, "especially when you study me like that."

"Ah, Kasey, what's with you? I said I was sorry." Michael had been particularly quiet this morning.

"Oh, I know, I know. I just wish . . . oh, never mind. Look, I'm sorry. OK?"

"Yes, it's ok, Kasey, best thing you can do is talk about it. Shall I get my notebook?"

Kathryn gave him an injured look. "I hope you don't think this is some wonderful, dramatic, one act play, Michael. You have no idea the sordid things that man is capable of doing. He used to tell me things when I was a small child. I didn't understand. I just knew they were awful."

"What things, Kasey? Honest, doll; I'm intrigued."

Kathryn flinched, "Please, Michael, don't call me 'doll'." Something black, like an invisible dark shroud seemed to fall over her. "Come on, Michael, I just don't want to talk. Let's get to work."

Kathryn talked the script down. She folded herself into it, smaller and smaller. She felt her real self shrink away as the crazy other person took hold. Her timing was perfect. "Don't hit me, please, Daddy, don't hit me." The script began to blur as her mind ran out of her. "I can't see . . . . lights too hot." Her voice came out in a tiny plea. She swallowed. It's ok . . . ok . . . keep going. He's angry." She paused and began again, "Please, Daddy, please. Oh, please, Daddy, give me back my doll?" She had no trouble making it real. Why did it matter so, that line? Why the vivid picture of the doll? The beautiful doll face seemed to emerge from the window opposite her, no longer a mental image, but real. "It's real," Kathryn said the words out loud. "It is real." She reached out to touch the yellow hair, the filmy gown. "Your gown is gone? Where? Oh, look, look at you. You're naked." She remembered for one tiny space, a flashback. It was him. His hands were moving quickly, a primitive motion.

"Wouldn't you like to play with the doll, Kathryn?" The words rang down on her. He held the doll out to her while his other hand jerked feverishly. "Here's your doll, Kathryn. Take her. She wants you." Kathryn saw the doll turned upside down, its hair falling over its head, hanging into the air. A wet ooze glazed its smooth, rubber body. The lights played down, Kathryn watched herself from somewhere else. She was in agony.

"I can't help her," she wailed. "I am stapled here." She spun around and left the chair as it whirled on its base, round and round. Michael's body shot at her through the swinging doors as they made a clapping sound, flapping wildly, beating the air.

"Stop it, Kathryn," Michael was shouting at her. "Stop it." He grabbed for her and caught her as she threw herself into the wall. He moved with her down the plaster and onto the floor. His arms pressed into her in a tight restraint. "You're all right, Kasey, I have you. It's ok, Kasey, it's ok. You're home."

"Yes," she said, nodding her head. Up and down she nodded. "Yes, I am home, aren't I?" She shivered and trembled. "Yes, I am home, aren't I?"

A Terrible Parable

or   contaminated thinking

we've gift wrapped

a little emperor

he's on display   right there on the white house

lawn

if you go early   you can catch him in his

birthday suit

or maybe signing executive decisions   with an authoritative smirk

ignoring the

checks and balances   going around congressional

corners

not engaging

any minds in this display of   arrogance

aware that he was   as Ann Richards

said, born with a

silver foot in his mouth   he's still sucking

he can't help it   he's an embarrassment

galvanizing   nurturing xenophobia in the

smaller minds of the

religious zealots

demonizing

intelligence and

those who would play devil's advocate.

i just keep thinking of living in a

yellow submarine

listening to bay Buchanan's statement that we have a ball game

to get ready for while

the border outrage continues and

the crime of ignorance   dubae

Spanish rather than English   and the united states

being run by a bunch of   hot johnsons

oh yeah   worried about their performances

meanwhile i am reminded of the barriers between

art and life   forever being

defiled by the narrow drawings of the engineers

and forgetting the

importance   of   a Rauchenberg

or duchamp

a   schwitter   kutzpah

your small pointed head

The Goose

Diane said the owl had torn the back of her neck off so she picked her up and gently carried her into the house. She laid her into the tub in the bathroom and made a poultice and put it over the back of her neck. . . over the wound. She talked to Diane while she ministered to her and the next morning Diane went apprehensively into the room expecting to find her dead but she was still alive and seemingly better. By afternoon, however, she was worse. Diane knew she was dying and sat in the bathroom floor patiently, waiting for her to die. Barbara came in and Diane noticed Tillie's face was wet. Tillie was crying and Diane began wiping her face with a clean cloth. . . Diane began weeping, too, sobbing louder and louder, trying to muffle her heartbreak, "please go get her mate" she said to Barbara, then, "no, we must carry her to him so they can be together". They wrapped her in a towel and carefully carried her down the back stairs into the barnyard. He huddled over her, talking to her. She talked back to him and tears continued to course down her face.

Later, Diane said that Tillie's mate hates her now as though he thinks she had something to do with destroying Tillie. He used to follow along beside Diane, nipping at her ankles, talking and playing. He will fertilize other female geese but they mate for life and he won't have anything to do with the other female geese in terms of companionship. Human beings think they are the only beings that do that. Think about it.

Diesel

Diesel, the raccoon, would come at dinner time and gobble up all the scraps we put out for her. We had cut a hole in the back entrance to the garage so she could get in and she would come every evening for her share of food. Other animals soon began coming as well . . . a fragile red fox, other raccoons, a skunk. . . we had a veritable zoo in our garage every evening. Diesel was the head honcho and loved to be invited into the kitchen to visit her old haunts, places she had discovered while still a little raccoon. She was still afraid of Conductor the cat and would show her distrust by biting at my ankles or running behind the washing machine. She would stand in the corner on her hind legs and scoot behind the screen door and expose her belly. She later brought her brood, chortling and moving as a group into the safety of our porch or into the garage. We could hear them late at night as they lived out their nocturnal existence. It went on like that until after Harmon died and then, one night, they never came again. I found them after the big snow, dead at the back of the house.

Ruminations

It's Spring and I am thinking about planting something in my garden, something in yellow or green. Plants make me so happy and I think of them with a great deal of love and appreciation but I had never thought much about green flowers until I saw something in one of Martha Stewart's editions. It was a profusion of green flowers and foliage and it was gloriously Martha. She is a genius and I love her. I don't know why people are so filled with anger and jealousy about Martha except that they are probably just vile little minds devoted to all that is less than and can't stand the beautiful things that Martha introduces into our lives. Some people are just devoid.

Anyway, my home is a cluttered collection, a myriad of objects I have gathered to me over the years. It is a picture of my life which is somewhat extemporaneous and given to pleasing me. It's a private place where I cook and dream, make art, and do a lot of writing.

I live a mostly simple life without many callers or parties because I prefer not being social or "out there". I am not a clubby as I call it though I have been a member of a few organizations as being alone all the time becomes unhealthy. We did join a church family once and that became frightening . The minister was a wonderful man but he had temper tantrums and his wife left him, the organ player was having affairs all the time, and many of the women in the church body were vying for the title of Queen of the church and I was overcome with feelings of outrage which I don't like. Anything that makes me feel outraged is a warning of imminent danger. . . it's kind of like the feelings I experience with groups of people. I wonder why people are so in need of a group to back their feelings, why are they so afraid to stand up on their own two feet. Smacks of groups of wolves and coyotes. This thing with Martha was probably conjured up by a group of men who were jealous and vindictive. Makes me think of green.

The trip to Europe

The trip to Europe was basically terrible. One should know better than to travel in summer. It was like being aboard a passenger ship while on its way down. My husband, who had never been up the Eiffel Tower, decided that a good idea. Try to imagine. When we finally got down after being stuffed into an elevator in unseasonably hot weather with a gathering of undeodorized humanity, the French man who was operating the lift, opened the door and in a great bellowing voice, shouted in English, "PLEASE, Get OUT".

Our German experience was, per usual, sour . . . . kraut. After being plied with green sauce, boiled chops and apple wine for several days, my intestines needed a rest. Our German friend who is a comedian, punned every statement I made. One such oral stab came when I remarked that those funny little Japanese friends would fit into one's pocket. My friend said, "yeah, den you would haf a pocket calculator".

We went on to tell him we had gotten on the train in Koln to travel to Frankfurt and our train split taking us off in another direction from our intended destination. We ended up getting off in a small town near Mainz. We went into the station and found a restaurant which was not serving food during the hours after lunchtime. Finally, a waitress approached me and in broken English (I can't speak a word of German) informed me that she would find something in the kitchen for us as we were starved.

When she brought the plates to the table, she began conversing and told us she was there to help her brother who ran the restaurant. She said he was dying and needed her for a while. She then went on to say that her Father, Mother, and Husband had also died recently and that her son had expired as well. It was sad though she didn't seem unhappy. After being told this story, our German friend raised an eyebrow and queried, "did dey eat der?"

One of his other observations interested me. As we sat at lunch eating some really awful version of Pizza, I inquired of the time. As we were on a schedule, we had to finish rapidly and pay our check. The waiter who had kept us waiting for a long period of time prior to taking our order, seemed to swoop down upon us in great haste, grab the money, and split. Our German friend said, "well, dis is interesting, he comes slow and leaves fast". I pondered that for some time.

Later that day, he dumped me out on the street so he and my husband could make a business call. The street seemed a little dirty and it was very hot. I went into a Perfumerie and began testing all the odors. After a while, I got a little nauseous and ventured out onto the street again only to be approached by several men as I glided down the way in front of theatres offering "peep" shows and sexy films. When I finally caught up with my companions, Andy, our German Friend, upon hearing my tale of ogling men, said, "if you go in the red light district, don't wear perfume".

The Way Things Work

She stood outside on the landing, staring down at him. He was always there at that time of day, smoking. The smoke rose up around his head and twirled off. "He's drawing a circumference," she thought, "and pulling me into it." He called out to her but she didn't understand his words. They were lost, whirling away like the smoke. She ran down the stairs to him, eagerly. "What were you saying? I didn't hear you."

"Oh, just a comment about the heat. It scours me today."

"That's an interesting way to put it. I prefer winter myself, it's so cozy.

"You find the winter cozy?"

"Oh, don't mind me, I'm always cold . . . especially my hands."

"Oh?"

"Yes." She reached over and touched her little finger to the railing, just touching it slightly. "My hands never work right. They seem to have their own life . . . quite independent of mine."

The sun was hot and the wood on the railing was warm. She bent her face over it feeling the heat rise, warming her face. She didn't look at him.

"What?" He bellowed

She was startled. "I was just enjoying the warm sun."

She blurted her next question, "Would you like to come Sunday and see my glass ladies?"

"Glass ladies?"

"Yes, some of my friends are coming and I was going to bring them out. It's a collection. There are all kinds of them. . . the glass ladies, I mean."

"Sunday? What time?"

"About one." Her hands were cold again. She laid them on the railing. "The only way I can get them warm is to take a bathe. I like to bathe or sit in the hot tub because it's so soothing. Warm water is just so soft." She looked directly into his eyes. His gaze met hers and held.

"I would like very much to see your glass ladies. I've never known anyone who collected such a thing." He pushed his cigarette through the crack in the wood.

"I know. It's very unusual." She rushed on. "They're hard to find. I look for them everywhere. Shop keepers don't like selling them. They break too easily. They're very expensive, you know."

"I expect they are." Their eyes locked. Neither spoke. A spider swung off a branch and laid a white line across the wood. "Are they clear?"

"Yes," she replied, "they have no color other than what they reflect. They're just pure crystal. The light does beautiful things in them and they sometimes look as though they are moving. It all depends on the light."

His eyes grew soft. "You are a funny little thing."

"Uh-huh. We'll have drinks and finger food. Do you want to bring your wife? Please do."

His eyes changed. He looked down at her hands. She followed

his gaze. Her veins were sticking up, all blue and pathetic looking. "I don't like parties much but I think we can come up Sunday. My wife needs a little diversion. Will there be many people here?"

"I really don't know. I just sort of asked around. . . different people. It should be interesting. It will be just an assortment of people. They're all nice."

"I'm sure," he said and lit another cigarette. "How many of these ladies do you have?"

"About fifteen. I broke one once. My hands were wet. I was polishing them and one just slipped from me. I couldn't hold her. I just had to let her drop. That's how it is with them."

He was drawing on his cigarette, listening. "I suppose if you squeeze them or grab at them they can break."

"Yes, that's it. She shattered all over the floor. I cut myself quite badly. Little cuts all over, not deep, but it was really bloody. The pieces were so small. I just wanted to pick it all up."

"Did you get all of it?"

"No, in the end, I had to suck it all up into the vacuum. You can imagine."

"It must have been disappointing."
"I cried."

He cocked his head and frowned, "Oh, you cried?"

"Yes, I cried for a long time. Do you ever cry?"

He smiled, "Old men don't cry very often." A fatherly tone crept into his voice, "but then I've never dropped a glass lady before."
"You probably wonder how I could cry over a piece of broken glass."

"No, no, it's your collection. Prices are high."

"It's more than that. It started out to be a hobby. Now I spend a lot of time looking at them. It's really strange but I find them to be good company."
"Yes, I suppose, but they can't talk."

"No, I don't talk very well either." Loneliness settled over her. "I have to go. I have to make some dinner for later." She paused and turned, remembering something. "Do you like petit fours?"

"I don't think I've ever eaten any."

"You haven't? They are a French confection. We'll have some on Sunday." She raised her hand as she left. "ta ta" At the landing she turned. He was looking up at her. From her higher place, he appeared bent as though she were viewing him through a piece of heavy glass. She could see his eyes glowing up at her. He raised his hand but continued to lean on the railing and stare at her.

She ran to the door marked, Taylor Sanger.

She fussed over the glass collection, lifting one then the other. "It's almost time, my ladies. Soon you will no longer be my secret." She set the last one down on the chest. "I am off to the kitchen, now, to make coffee." She busied herself with wiping the teacups, lining them up neatly next to the white, linen napkins. "I will take this one candle in for them. They look so pretty with the candle behind them." She set the white taper into the silver candlestick holder and carried it into the living room. "Yes, just behind you," she muttered, "it will warm your poor bodies." She carefully set the candle in its place behind the lucid shapes. "I do hope no one will touch you. I don't want their fingers on you." She grimaced. There was a tap on the door.

"Oh, Lilly, do come in. So good of you to come."

"Hello, Sweets. Roger will be up. He's parking the car. Oh, my, there they are. They are so beautiful, Tay. How lovely." Lilly lowered her voice as she hovered over the delicate shapes. The finish on the brown chest glistened. The ladies' shadows cast strange forms against the grain in the wood. The candle sent the tall willowy shapes onto the wall behind them.

"Hello," Roger walked through the open door.

"Roger, come in and say hello to the ladies."

Tay stood with her hands folded in front of her. Her tiny waist was held tightly with a wide, taut belt. "Would you like some coffee?"

"Yes, that would be . . . someone else is arriving, dear. Oh, hello,

Carol. Come on in. Come see Tay's ladies. They are just beautiful."

Several people were milling around the door. Others were arriving. "I do think this is fun, Taylor. How do you keep them so clean. It must be a huge risk."

"Yes, she is, isn't she? Delightful little apartment."

"Where did you say you got those. . . ?"

" . . . and two of them had nothing on at all."

"It was so warm. You'd think the . . . Tay, there's some interesting man out here in the hall."
"We really must have lunch, Tay. You and I are so much alike."

"Someone took all four of them. Just took them. I could hardly believe it."

Taylor walked in from the kitchen. He was standing at the glass collection, studying them. The woman had her back to the kitchen door. "It's them." Taylor moved quickly into the room and up behind the thin female figure. "You must be Mrs. Tome,

I am so glad you came. Did you see the glass ladies?"

"Yes, they are lovely," her eyes were wide with something like a question. She looked very intently at Tay. "Please call me Sharon."

"Oh, may I? Your husband and I exchange small talk frequently. I thought you might enjoy meeting my glass ladies."

"Yes, they are lovely," she repeated the former statement. "I need to get out more, the pressure at the office is just awful." She jerked her head around in the direction of the glass collection. "Dan was interested in seeing what you have here."

Someone called across the room, "Tay, my goodness, these are so fragile."

"Yes, aren't they?" She swept into the center of the room. "I think we should light the candle now. It's gone out." Her hands shook. "Cold," she whispered. She lifted the match and lighted the candle. Little bullets of wax sizzled off onto the crystal skirt of the nearest figure. "Oh, look what I have done."

"Can I help?" He cupped his hand around her elbow and

pressed. Tay turned and looked into his warm, liquid eyes. Something moved inside her. He reached for the matches, "your hands are so cold. Are you nervous?" His were warm and soft. "No, no, no. They're always cold. I told you that yesterday. Don't you remember?"

He glanced over at his wife who was talking with a tall, blonde woman with blue eyes. "This is very interesting. I should have something with me . . . a pencil or something to write with."

"That's an odd thing. Why a pencil?"

"Oh, I collect information. My writing, you know. Your women friends are all so fair and you are so dark. The light is moving in the ladies. They seem to talk."

"Of course, I know. The conversations we don't hear." She trembled. "They are so noisy, aren't they? I'm afraid she knows."

"Yes she has good eyes and she sees things."
Lilly walked up to them. "Tay, I want you to see Roger's house. The one where he grew up. You'd so enjoy it. It's an old

Victorian."

"Really, Lilly, how nice."

"Perhaps we could drive to Chicago and have a look sometime? I need the rest and you and I simply must spend some time together, Tay. Lilly pressed a cup of hot coffee into her palm. "Lilly, have you met Mr. Tome, Dan, he's my neighbor." Carol sallied over with Jerry, her new bed partner. "Guess what, Tay? Jerry has booked some of your friends for another cooking class. It's bone marrow soup this week."

"Oh, I can't abide the thought of eating an animal much less boiling their bones."

"Oh, well, we don't want to offend you and your sensitive feelings about animals, dear, it's just that most people do eat animal flesh and Jerry offers these classes in how to do it appropriately."

Gordon, Tay's attorney, was looking over his glasses at the crystal formations and a smile played around his lips. His young wife stared at the ladies intently. He turned to her, "Look, Cookie, look at how they seem to curtsey. Their skirts look like pedals."

Tay smiled as she watched them. Their exchanges were intimate and important. "Gordon is such the perfect cavalier," she thought. "His lady is la pièce de résistance but not at all like glass." Aloud, she whispered, "Porcelain."

"Did you say something, Tay?" Gordon's eyes danced as he looked at her.

"No," she responded simply. "Oh, look at that!" Tay extended a small, blue hand. The candle flame was weaving, swaying, the ladies seem to twirl, softly. One held a tiny flower, each petal a perfect statement. The light cast a motion into the glass arms offering the flowers. Tay curtsied with mock sincerity and backed away toward the kitchen. She began another pot of coffee.

The steam rose out of the spout. She stood with her hands raised over it, feeling the wet warmth seep into her hands. Dan sacheted in. "Are you free this evening?" His eyes made a half-arc, avoiding hers. "Sharon is making a check run to the office."

She didn't reply.

"Well, what time is it over?"

"I don't know. Sh-shortly. I'm tired." She giggled nervously.
Her eyelids fluttered. She saw the twitch under his glasses. "I'll
be here, I'll wait."

He twisted the gold ring on his finger, "this is all new to me. I've
never done this sort of thing before."

"I can't imagine why you should. She is really lovely. I am
flattered. No, I am. What's wrong?"

"I'm scared." He looked at her for a long moment. "You
understand, don't you?"
"Understand?"

"Yes, I was thinking about a place in Paris. I could write and
you could make petit fours and play. . . you know, play?"

"It would be nice. We could go to the Luxembourg Gardens on
Sunday and watch the children sail their little boats on the
fountains or dance around amid the flowers."

He looked at her appealingly. She sighed. "Things don't work
out that way, do they? It's just a vision, a silly diversion like my
glass ladies. I can watch the world move in them in a silent

171

cacophony of colored lights. It's all just color and movement, bumping around in a clear womb."

"Someone is calling you." He said. She watched his eyes as she brushed by him. They were full of pain and wonder.

"I am so glad you came."

"Perfectly lovely, Tay."

"Remember what I said about Chicago."

"Yes, Lilly."

"You all right, Tay? You look a little pale."

"Yes, fine, thanks. See you tomorrow."

Great little thing you had here, Tay."

"Thank you, Gordon, so glad you could come." Tay kissed Cookie.

"Lunch soon, Tay?"

"Good, yes, we'll do that."

"Bye, Carol, nice seeing you, Jerry. Do stop by soon."

Dan and Sharon Tome waited, smiling. "We'll be going, too.
Thank you for asking us," Sharon spoke.
"Yes, Taylor, thank you. Nice Sunday."
"I'm here. Come anytime." He nodded.

"Later," he said quietly.

Taylor walked back into the room and began collecting cups and
napkins. The saucers rattled in her hands as she deposited them
on the drain board. She walked back into the living room and
sat opposite the collection. A quiet time passed. The candle
flame still flirted with the air. The night was pumping up. Tay's
eyes traveled to the door. There was a soft tap. "Come in," She
said it as if it were a comment. The door opened and Dan
stepped in. He clasped the inside door knob and closed the
door.

"You're still with your ladies?"

"Yes."
He walked over and sat beside her. He extended his hands and
she laid her small ones into them. "They are still cold," he said.

The light from the candle spun around them. The flame grew upward. Its color seized the glass skirts of the mute ladies and began swaying in their bodies. The room cooled and breathed. Her hand lay on his arm now. Her wrist bent to brush against his skin. He laid his own warm hand against the small place at her waist. The ladies seemed to raise in the glow, smiles frozen into their glass faces. The one still extended a flower. . . sans peur et sans reproche.

Some non-fiction

In 2003, my husband and I decided to take a product to market which his father had designed in the 1940's and never marketed. At the time, we lived in California and contacted a person in the Sacramento area who proceeded to charge lots of money, take the product to China for molds and manufacture, take control of the production process, and leave us out of the loop. We were totally dependent on him and he kept our money for over a year as we waited for product.

Finally, we received our product after we had moved to Tucson and I began an investigation of where to go to have it made here. I began with one company and met an individual in the field of graphics who put me onto good manufacturing facilities. We moved through the process of retrofitting molds, finding packaging facilities, and redoing our graphics, etc.

We are still in business, building customer base, and servicing that base. Point is: People in the USA CAN DO and at a reasonable price. It is also less stressful.

I think Americans deserve to know that all this is possible and I hope you would get this information to them.

I am available for questions, comments, and furthering dreams. I am an American.

myra fairchild

thecheeseknife.com

myrafairchild@thecheeseknife.com

520-829-7449 • fax: 520-829-7415

Tara

Myra

Sabra

Riley and Zander

wedding day

glamour girl

Myra at Stonehenge